cell

A Play in Two Parts
for Four Actors and a Voice

cell

A Play in Two Parts
for Four Actors and a Voice

Paula Meehan

NEW ISLAND

First published in Ireland in September 2000
by New Island Books
2 Brookside
Dundrum Road
Dublin 14

A CIP catalogue record for this book is available from the British
Library

ISBN 1 902602 38 2

The Arts Council
An Chomhairle Ealaíon

New Island Books receives financial assistance from The Arts Council
(An Chomhairle Ealaíon), Dublin, Ireland.

Caution

Typeset by New Island Books
Printed in Ireland by Betaprint
Cover design by Slick Fish Design, Dublin
Cover Image by PCC, Dublin

for Garrett Keogh

Cell was commissioned by Calypso Theatre Company who mounted a production of it in the City Arts Centre, Dublin. It was first performed there on the sixth of September, 1999. The cast were:

MARTHA CASEY	Barbara Bergin
LILA BYRNE	Laura Brennan
ALICE KANE	Joan Sheehy
DELORES ROCHE	Eithne McGuinness
VOICE	Lisa Tierney-Keogh

Set Design	Robert Ballagh
Lighting Design	Paul Keogan
Costume Design	Marie Tierney
Sound	Ray Duffy
Production Manager	Marie Tierney
Stage Manager	Paula Tierney *with* Casey Norton
Assistant Stage Manager	Conor Mullen

Directed by Garrett Keogh

For Calypso Productions:
Artistic Director, Bairbre Ní Chaoimh
Company Manager, Maria Fleming
Administrative Assistant, Aoife Conroy.

Characters

DOLORES ROCHE: Dublin woman, 42 years old. Seven-year sentence for dealing in heroin. Four years served.

MARTHA CASEY: Dublin woman, 26 years old. Four-year sentence for shoplifting. Two years and three months served.

LILA BYRNE: Dublin woman, 19 years old. Three-year sentence for possession of heroin. One year and one month served.

ALICE KANE: Leitrim woman, 49 years old. Life sentence for murder. Just beginning her sentence.

VOICE: Neutral female.

Time

Part 1 — October Full Moon

Part 2 — November Full Moon

Part One

Cell. Back wall with door. Four metal bunks, two to each side, metal ladders at end of bunks to reach top bunks. Four metal lockers. Two metal chairs. One metal table, bolted to the floor, with tea making equipment — large flask with lock on it, milk, sugar, cups. Curtained off area to back with slop bucket, rubbish bin and sink. One barred window high up over top right-hand bunk. One central barred ceiling light, controlled from outside. One speaker in security cage high up on back wall. Intercom mouthpiece beside door.

Two top bunks and lower right bunk heavily decorated, adorned, individualised; dressed with duvets, sheeting, quilts all different; walls nearby plastered with photos, posters, postcards, personal effects. Other lower bunk stripped to mattress, institutional-looking sheets, blankets, pillows piled neatly on it. Walls around this bunk bare, though traces of Blu-tack and Sellotape remain. Three lockers decorated with personal effects, toiletries. Other locker bare.

It is the October Full Moon. Play opens on dim cell. Greenish glow from cell light. Dark outside. And very cold.

Delo Roche *in top bunk under window.* **Lila Byrne** *in bunk below her.* **Martha Casey** *in other top bunk which has a stiff white sheet of paper affixed to the wall nearby with days served of her four-year sentence marked off.*

Delo stirs and climbs down ladder. Goes into curtained area. Only sound her strong stream of piss into galvanised bucket.

DELO: Well fuck them anyway. Manky wagons. Which of them? Batman? Or Robin?

Delo comes out of curtained area with slop bucket. Puts it down noisily. Goes to each of sleepers in turn shaking them awake.

DELO: Rise and shine, little piggies. Mama sow has a bone to pick. A bone to pick? A bone to chew! With one of you.

MARTHA: What time is it? It can't be time to get up? I'm only gone over.

LILA: Yes. I'm coming, Delo. I'm coming.

Lila hurries out of bed. Stands shivering.

MARTHA: Leave me alone. I'm in the middle of a dream.

DELO: I'm getting to the bottom of this. Martha Casey, get out of that bed.

MARTHA: It's too cold. Go away.

DELO: When I say jump, I mean jump.

Delo drags Martha out of the bed by her hair. Stands her beside Lila. Puts bucket before them.

DELO: Whose is that?

MARTHA: What are you on about?

LILA: I don't know anything about it, Delo. Honestly.

MARTHA: Will someone tell me what's going on?

DELO: I'm waiting.

Silence.

DELO: I'm waiting.

Silence.

DELO: Don't try my patience. I want answers and I want them fast.

LILA: It wasn't me. I swear it.

MARTHA: Search me.

DELO: That's exactly what it may come to. One of you is early. One of you is out of sync with the heavenly cycle. Now. Which of you?

LILA: I want to go back to bed. I don't feel good.

DELO: Tough tittie, baby. Nobody goes anywhere, does anything, till this is sorted. Which of you?

Silence.

DELO: I have all day.

Martha *goes to sit.*

DELO: On your feet missus.

Delo *gets dressed.*

DELO: I'm in no hurry. You're in no hurry. Hah! We have all the time in the world. Now. We had a pact. Right? Don't interrupt! No blood. No faecal matter, or shit as it's known to you scumbags. A co-pi-ous supply of plastic bags in there. Couldn't be easier. This day and age. The big V. It makes sense. You know it does. Lila? Martha? Mar? Lila? It's the principle of the thing, really. A pact. A solemn, solemn promise. For the health of all. The good of the many. Basic hygiene. You do see? Martha? Lila? Martha? I'm waiting.

Silence.

DELO: I'm waiting.

MARTHA: Look Delo — we'll share the blame. If you're so bloody anxious to put it somewhere. It was both of us. Okay?

LILA: Yes. Yes.

DELO: A simple answer to a simple question. Who-done-it? Mystery.

Delo goes into cubicle.

MARTHA: I was having the weirdest dream. I was in me Ma's and I was looking for Jasmine. Me Ma was minding her for me, do you see? Only I couldn't find her anywhere and there was this strange smell coming from the kitchen. I went in and there was a pot on the gas boiling away like mad. I lifted the lid and there was Jasmine all chopped up. Like a lump of meat she was. There was a bit of her face with the eye; and then another chunk with her mouth; all rolling around in the boiling water. And do you know what I did? I turned the gas down to simmer and put the lid back on.

LILA: Stop, Martha.

Light comes on full. Loud buzzer for ten seconds then —

VOICE: *(From speaker)* — Your attention please. Your attention please. Slop out in fifteen minutes.

DELO: A new day has dawned comrades. According to the powers that be. Though nature has yet to get the message. The sun still sleeps. Cold enough for you?

LILA: Please. I'm frozen.

DELO: Yes. A new day. Work to be done. Deals to be struck. Profits to be made. And the drones mutinous. What did I do, I ask myself, to be lumbered with such incompetents?

MARTHA: Give us a break, Delo.

DELO: It's the principle of the thing. Fair trade. Hasn't that always been the motto? The family motto so to speak? Have I not been like a mother to you both? Ingrates.

MARTHA: You scratch my back and I'll …

DELO: Shut it!

LILA: Please. I don't feel good. I'm sick. I'm going to drop out of my standing.

MARTHA: Incriminate yourself, why don't you?

LILA: I'm just a bit dope sick. That's all. I'm cold.

MARTHA: I'm not feeling too good myself …

DELO: You could sing that if you had a tune *(Sings) I'm not feeling too good myself!*

Silence.

DELO: It's always just a question of time. Of biding one's time. Who will break first? For I believe in the one true apostolic church of God Almighty. Who has four hooves and a flying mane. Or a scaly body and he breathes fire. But cuddly none the less. Yes. I perceive my girlies want to cuddle up. Amn't I right?

LILA: Please …

DELO: Oh pretty please. Whiny now. I can hear the edge creep into your voice. Pleeeese. On your knees soon. No dope today girlies.

Silence.

DELO: So whose is it?

Silence.

DELO: Eh?

Delo grabs Lila by the hair and twists it.

DELO: Now. Who? Martha?

LILA: Stoppit!

DELO: Martha?

MARTHA: Lookit. I'm sorry Lila. It was Lila. OK? We'll be here all bleeding day. I just can't … It was her. We're better getting it over with.

LILA: No. I swear. Don't mind her, Delo.

DELO: Now we're getting places. I'm all ears.

MARTHA: I don't believe this is happening. What does it matter?

LILA: It was an accident. On me Ma's life. I shouldn't be bleeding till next week. I didn't know they were going to come. I'm early.

DELO: You're too late.

LILA: No I'm early … please Delo. I really need something. To take the edge off.

DELO: Tried to lie to Mama. Who looks out for you, eh? Whose rules are simple and kind. Who takes umbrage at the thought that one of her girls would … attempted murder. That's what it is. Your blood Lila — riddled with the virus. Oh yes. Riddled. Look. (***Delo** pushes **Lila**'s head into bucket*)

MARTHA: Leave her, Delo. She's sick.

DELO: Some friend, you. You gave her away. Lamb to the slaughter.

VOICE: *(Preceded by chime)* Attention. Slop out now. Door opening in ten seconds.

DELO: Let's see. Who'll it be? Will it be thee? Or thee? My o me.

***Delo** looks meaningfully at door.*

LILA: Don't make me go out there. I can't … *(Cowering as far from door as she can get)*

DELO: Can't? Can't? Won't! You'll take that bucket and you'll scrub and polish till I can see my face in it.

MARTHA: Let me do it, Delo. You know she can't handle things out there.

DELO: Oh touching.

MARTHA: She hasn't crossed that threshold since Annie ...

DELO: And she expects me to keep her monkey fed. What am I — the Society for the Prevention of Cruelty to Animals? Never-ending source of peanuts? For her greedy monkey?

Door opens. Buzzer sounds while it's open.

DELO: Get the door Lila! Get the bucket Lila! If you don't get the bucket Lila, fuck it Lila, we're with the bucket all day.

Lila *doesn't move.*

DELO: You go so, Martha. Quick. And see who wants what. And remember the company motto — do not ask for credit as a refusal often offends.

*Exit **Martha** with bucket, black plastic rubbish bag and tea flask. **Delo** drags **Lila** back to standing position.*

DELO: Let's get a few things straight. You don't work, monkey doesn't get fed. Work. Let us consider work. You won't leave this cell. As a runner you're a write off. Martha's been holding up your end of the business besides her own. The work of two. Admittedly you've kept our little nest shipshape and spotless. Oh immaculate. You could eat your dinner off the floor. A gold-star skivvy you is, you is. But, me darling, it's not enough ...

LILA: I'm very cold.

DELO: That snot is not the morning chill.

LILA: Givvus something. Just enough to take the edge off ...

DELO: The famous, nay the notorious edge. Stop snivelling. I can't abide a whiner.

LILA: I'll do your corns.

DELO: Florence fucking Nightingale herself. Here.

Delo takes out home-made knife and gives it to **Lila***.*

LILA: I'll be real gentle.

DELO: Crippled I am.

LILA: Every cripple has a way of dancing. Do you remember Annie used say that?

DELO: You mark my words — avoid high heels. He-highls. That's what my girls would call them. When they were only little. They'd dress up in my old stuff and ... Ah fuck it. Nobody knows what I go through with these feet of mine. Martyred I am.

LILA: I feel all weird. I'd another dream about Annie. She was here in the cell with us again. Begging ...

DELO: Very apt. Considering her background.

LILA: She said she had no peace where she was.

DELO: Beware the restless dead. They wander the earth ...

LILA: Stop.

DELO: ... forever.

LILA: She begged me to get her dug up out of her grave. She said ...

Delo takes knife back off Lila and puts it away.

DELO: Suicides never have peace. It's us haunt them. Not letting them rest. Do you understand? *(Shaking her)*

LILA: She ... she ... *(Sobbing)*

DELO: Let her go. Let her rest in peace. That's enough now. Get a grip. I forbid the mention of her name. Do you understand?

Silence.

DELO: Here. We were talking payment. Fair exchange being no robbery.

Delo goes to unused bunk. Lies back and beckons Lila over. Lila begins to fondle Delo. Brings her to climax. As this happens —

DELO: Snuggle in there. Oh yes. That's the spot. X marks the spot. Sex marks the spot. O I like that. There. That's good. And Snakey likes it too! Talking down the neck of her sweatshirt. You like this don't you Snakey. Yes. Yes. Faster now. Yes. Hi ho hi ho it's off to work we go, go, go, go. Snakey loves it. Yes . Lovely. Lovely. Lovely.

Delo and Lila lie curled in each other's arms. Sun comes up and window lightens as Delo's breathing goes back to normal.

DELO: Who's my girl?

LILA: I am Delo.

DELO: This is nice, isn't it?

LILA: It's great Delo.

DELO: Won't I mind you?

LILA: Yes Delo.

DELO: Who's your best pal?

LILA: You are Delo. Any chance ...

Delo puts finger to lip. Silence. They drift.

LILA: And Delo?

DELO: Wha?

LILA: I'm sorry. About the blood ...

DELO: De nada. De nada.

LILA: Delo, I'm in a bad way.

Buzzer sounds and door opens. Enter **Martha** *with breakfast tray including tea flask, and cleaned bucket on her arm. Puts breakfast on table.*

MARTHA: How sweet. Yis're like a picture.

Martha takes bucket back to cubicle. She lays out breakfast. Then puts scrunched up bundle of notes on table while —

MARTHA: Fourteen orders, Delo. Eight paid in advance. Two in kind. Halfzware shag, five packs, duty free; and a pair of gold earrings. Is that okay? Seemed like a good deal to me. They *are* gold as far as I can tell. Look there's a stamp on them. The rest — cash on delivery. Which I promised would be this lunchtime. That wagon Miriam ... with the funny eye. You never know if she's looking at you or behind you. I keep looking over her shoulder and then she says, 'Who are you looking at?'. Jee-sus.

Delo and Lila rise. Delo gets nodge of heroin from slit in mattress where she keeps her stash. Lila burns it on tinfoil and sucks up smoke through biro. Lila goes to cubicle where she washes and dresses.

MARTHA: Happy families again, is it?

DELO: *(Giving* **Martha** *her nodge)* Well done, o faithful servant. Get that into you girl!

MARTHA: There's talk we'll have a new one. In here.

DELO: Oh yeah?

MARTHA: Wait for it. A murderer.

DELO: You mean a murderess.

MARTHA: What? That's what I heard anyway. She stabbed a guy. Dead.

DELO: A real criminal at last. Thank God. I'm surrounded by puddycats.

MARTHA: *(Smoking)* I feel human again. That's a lovely bit of gear.

DELO: So ...

MARTHA: So?

DELO: So what did you find out about her. Our murderess?

MARTHA: That's it. No one knows her. The bandy-legged screw told Rose Bourke. And this is the only spare bed on the wing. So.

DELO: So.

MARTHA: I'd say she'd be cool. Hey Lila. We've someone for Annie's bunk. A murderer.

LILA: I wouldn't sleep in that bunk.

MARTHA: That's rich after what I walked in on. Give us a break.

LILA: It's different. Annie died in that bunk.

DELO: Her name wasn't to be mentioned in this cell again. Remember? We're making a fresh start. Clean slate. Capisco? Let the dead R.I.P.

Delo *counts money. Stashes it. Goes to wash.*

MARTHA: You should eat.

LILA: Me stomach's in bits.

MARTHA: You're as thin as a rake. Are you sure? (*Taking Lila's portion*) Thanks.

LILA: Who did she murder?

MARTHA: Her fellow. Stabbed him.

LILA: Jesus. Have you ever met a murderer before?

MARTHA: (*Nods to cubicle*) Not a convicted murderer. Just a certain person who got away with it.

DELO: (*Coming out of cubicle drying off*) Got away with what?

MARTHA: Got away with murder.

DELO: (*Coming to table and eating*) They're voting today. And guess what's the biggest issue in this election? Crime! Our speciality girruls. I hope you're proud. The papers are full of us. New prisons. That's what the sheep are being promised. Ha. We're their worst nightmare. They want us kept well off the streets. Make them safe for peace and reconciliation.

LILA: I hope she's not rough.

DELO: Ooh Miss Dainty-Tainty toes. I hehope shehes nawth rouhehef.

MARTHA: Or common. I can't abide a common woman.

DELO: Bad language!

MARTHA: She picks her nose!

DELO: And eats it!

LILA: It's just if she's a psycho or something.

DELO: In with us norms.

MARTHA: Us upstanding members of the community.

DELO: Write to your TD why don't you? Make it an election issue. Sure she might corrupt you. *(Delo fondles Lila's breast)* Innocent yang thang. Do you like that? *(Opens her shirt and begins to sex her up)* You do. You like it. Are you getting jealous Martha? Mammy loves Lila. Mammy loves her little titties.

MARTHA: Climbing to her bunk to scratch another day off her sentence chart — Yis're disgusting.

DELO: You weren't saying that last week. I wasn't a bit disgusting then. *(Losing interest in Lila)* Right. I want to sort a few things out ...

MARTHA: I said I'd fix them up at lunchtime.

DELO: Excellent. It must be nearly morning visiting. Deliveries! Deliveries! *(Buzzer sounds)* — on the button.

VOICE: Visit for Dolores Roche. Dolores Roche.

Buzzer sounds and door opens.

DELO: Be good now.

Exit Delo.

LILA: I feel sick. I'm going to have to wash myself again.

MARTHA: Go way out of that. You were lapping it up. You like it.

LILA: The idea makes me want to throw up. Jesus.

MARTHA: Who are you trying to cod. Oh, she made me do it. Oh, I had to do it for a bit of gear. You should see your face. All dreamy and …

LILA: *(Climbing up to window at **Delo***'s *bunk)* I've no choice in the matter.

MARTHA: You're taking your life in your hands up there.

LILA: Fuck her. I only want a look.

MARTHA: I thought you were agir … agriphonic. You won't even take your visits.

LILA: Looking is different, but. I could spend the rest of me natural looking out a window.

MARTHA: There's little enough to see out there.

LILA: You're wrong, Martha. It's the humour of the day as much as anything. Today is … sulky. There are big black clouds away over where the canal would be. Jesus Martha, it's beautiful — there's a full moon up. In the daytime, imagine. Isn't that a brilliant thing. It's like you can look right through it. And it's been raining in the night. The roofs are all black and glittery. There's two more cranes on the site for the new prison. It's flying up. Do you think we'll be in be Christmas? I heard we'll be in be Christmas. There's a woman pushing a child in a buggy passing the end of the lane. And a dog. Sniffing. Ah cocking his leg at the wall. He's off after … maybe he's with the woman who passed. It was like someone called to him. And there's the edge of that big tree. The weeping willow in the back garden at the other end. Very sad looking. The leaves beginning to fall. Yellow they are now. Annie loved that tree. And I can see the top-half of a lamppost with the election poster with your woman's face on it … wait a minute … A New Ireland. Forward to … something. I can't make it out. I wish I could see more of the garden. The bit of the tree is the only growing thing. No. There's stuff on the wall.

Weeds. In the cracks. They had a little blue flower in ...
June, was it? Before ...

MARTHA: Wow. Epic! It's a useless view.

LILA: No. Don't say that.

MARTHA: The other side you can see the mountains.
Jesus Christ but it's cold. Look at me fingers. They're blue.

LILA: I don't see how they'd have the new prison ready be
Christmas?

MARTHA: I wouldn't start packing, that's for sure.

LILA: I dreamt of Annie again.

Silence.

LILA: She was there in front of me as large as life.

MARTHA: Will you leave it rest?

LILA: 'It's cold here. And lonely. Help me.' That's what
she said. She was wearing that colourdy cardigan and a
denim skirt.

MARTHA: Knacker clothes.

LILA: Traveller.

MARTHA: Knacker.

LILA: A knacker is someone who makes glue out of dead
animals.

MARTHA: She told you that.

LILA: So.

MARTHA: She wouldn't speak to the rest of us.

LILA: Yis gave her a terrible time. It's no wonder she wouldn't speak to you.

MARTHA: She was an awful eejit.

LILA: I miss her.

MARTHA: She had you wrapped around her little finger. The recyclers! According to you they should've been getting fucking medals for collecting scrap. Will you ever forget Delo and the constipation? Massive constipation she had. I don't think she shat the whole time Annie was here.

LILA: That wasn't Annie's fault.

MARTHA: She got very weird about Annie. A tin of Andrews a day she was on.

LILA: She was always going on about the smell. She made Annie wash down the whole cell twice a day. Yis didn't understand Annie. Yis never bothered your arses talking to her. She was very hurt.

MARTHA: Do you remember the day Delo sat with the clothespeg on her nose?

LILA: Stop. Don't be mocking her. I think she can hear us. I'm serious. I feel her very close.

MARTHA: Where is she? Up in the fucking air vent?

Silence.

MARTHA: Anyway even if she hadn't died Delo was fixing to get her moved. One of the screws owed her one. One of the screws always owes her one. Isn't that how Delo operates? Hah? You'd want to watch it or you'll end up with Tracy fucken Dunne farting in your face while you suck her off. You'd love that, wouldn't you? Delo's not the worst.

Silence.

MARTHA: Lila? I'm sorry about ratting on you.

Silence.

MARTHA: You'd still be freezing in your nightgear if I hadn't a told her. What was it the last time? She made us stand in our bare feet for thirty bleedin hours.

LILA: Yeah.

MARTHA: That's only last month. I've it marked in. You can't see from there. You'd need to be right up close. A little cross by the side. A cross for the bad days. And a star for the good ones.

LILA: I didn't know I was going to start bleeding. I'm very early.

MARTHA: They're me red dot days. Regular as clockwork.

LILA: I'm up in a heap. Me system is gone haywire.

MARTHA: That's Annie for you. The shock. It'll all calm down. You'll be grand. If you'd only make the effort.

Silence.

LILA: I don't think I'm going to make it.

MARTHA: Give over that class of talk.

Silence.

MARTHA: You should make the chart. Use the back of one of your posters.

LILA: No.

MARTHA: Why not? It'd give you something to do. Tick off the days. You could see where you stood.

LILA: I've a year and eleven months to go. Or thereabouts. I've a third served. Just over. I don't know, but. I like to forget. Let the weeks go by and then one day add it up. For the surprise.

Silence.

LILA: Where did the chart get Annie. You had *her* at it and look where she is now.

MARTHA: Forget it. Forget I mentioned it. Right.

LILA: She only had three months left.

MARTHA: Do your time whatever way you fucking-well like!

Buzzer sounds for opening door. **Lila** *jumps from bunk, anxiously smoothing duvet cover.*

LILA: Christ, it's warm where I was sitting.

MARTHA: Leave it, quick!

Enter **Alice Kane***.*

LILA: Jaysus. I thought you were Delo. Me heart!

ALICE: I'm Alice Kane. How are ye?

They scrutinise her.

ALICE: This'll be my bed, will it?

MARTHA: I think there's been a mistake. We weren't … What I mean is … Who sent you here?

ALICE: That's a good one. The judge it was sent me. Same as yourselves no doubt.

MARTHA: I mean we were expecting someone else.

ALICE: The Queen of Sheba, was it? *(Half under her breath, singing) The fair Aurora, or the goddess Flora.*

MARTHA: It's just that we were told someone else was coming.

ALICE: Ye have the place lovely, I'll give ye that. Tea and all. Sure this is grand. I didn't know what to expect.

LILA: Will you have a cup? We should've offered.

ALICE: That'd be great, child.

LILA: *(Pouring tea)* I'm Lila. Lila Byrne. Martha Casey. And Delo's on a visit. Delo Roche. It's short for Dolores.

ALICE: Lila. Now don't be telling me. That'd be short for Delilah? Am I right?

MARTHA: Delilah. Jesus.

LILA: Just Lila. It's Indian. My Ma was into a lot of Indian stuff when she had me. In London.

ALICE: Ah, a Londoner. There's plenty from round my part of the world over beyond. The McGuigan boys are in Cricklewood. And the Reynolds all upped and off to Croydon. As sudden as you like. Owed the bank, do you see? And the Earley daughter left only this summer to go studying. Newcastle, I think. Up north. Was your father an Indian man then?

MARTHA: Her Da's from Crumlin.

LILA: An Indian! That's gas. I was only four weeks in London and me Ma moved back. Me Da stayed. I've never set eyes on him. But me Ma was way into all the Indian stuff — meditation, the Guru.

MARTHA: *(Skitting)* Hari, hari. Wiggy woo dja! Gumbo gombo, have a sambo. Chicken Tikka.

LILA: *(Joining in old routine)* Jambo, jambo, onion bhagee. Don't mind her missus.

ALICE: And a beautiful name it is too. Now I'm Alice after my grandmother. She was from Fermanagh, out by Derrylin way. A McManus. The tribal chiefs of that place. I knew a Casey once. Had the hotel in Carrick, but sure it went to wrack and ruin. Too fond of the produce. God love him. A real gentleman.

MARTHA: Jesus. *(Mimicking)* A real gentleman.

LILA: Stop it.

MARTHA: Here Alice. What are you in for? Rustling? Is it? Or sheep shagging.

ALICE: Sheep! As a matter of fact I did keep a few sheep. Only the few, mind. The land is too wet. Christ, you could sell land by the bucket after the rain this summer. If you'd call it a summer.

LILA: Sugar? Milk?

MARTHA: Interfering with bulls, was it?

LILA: She's winding you up. Bulls!

MARTHA: Goats!

ALICE: Well I'll not be troubling you for long, for a bad mistake was made. Haven't I the new solicitor now and she says it's only a matter of time and they'll see I'm an innocent party.

MARTHA: *(Mimicking)* A bad mistake was made. Shurely it was. Amn't I after telling you.

LILA: She's an awful slagger. Here, you can use that locker and that's the cubicle for washing. It's the only bit of privacy you'll get. And the bucket …

MARTHA: The bucket is for doing the old one two. But there are rules. You'll be meeting Delo anon and she makes the rules.

LILA: Delo's a hard ticket. You'd want to watch yourself with her. We have to … well we have to …

MARTHA: It's simple. Use the bucket only for pissing. Then pour it down the sink and rinse out the bucket. If you have to shite, do it in a plastic bag. Tie it securely and put it in the rubbish bin. Or if you have your monthlies. Though I'd say … you're past it.

LILA: It's to cut down on the chance of infection. From the virus like.

ALICE: *(Baffled)* What? Well I'm sure I'll get the hang of it. I shouldn't be in here too long in any case. You make a great cup of tea, child.

MARTHA: Here, child, I've a mouth on me too.

ALICE: It's all relative. I feel like I'm about two thousand years old. I couldn't get a wink of sleep in the remand place. Most of this morning I spent sitting in a corridor waiting to be processed. Like a pea. Ha. A bit of company shortens the road. *(Looking round)* The pity I didn't bring a few photographs myself. Of my own boys. I've two sons. Fine boys. Never a minute's trouble. In America. And two grandchildren, a boy and a girl. One each. Four and six. Is that your daughter Martha? Isn't she a little dote? She has your eyes. And you Lila? No. Plenty of time yet.

MARTHA: That's Jasmine. She lives with his Ma. I won't let her be brought into this place.

ALICE: How long is it now since you've seen her?

LILA: Martha's in over two year …

ALICE: Would you not be afraid she'd forget who you are?

MARTHA: No fear. No fucking fear. She's as sharp as razors. Doing great in school.

ALICE: A beautiful child.

Door buzzer sounds.

VOICE: Solicitor to see Alice Kane. Alice Kane.

ALICE: What? What do …?

LILA: Quick now!

MARTHA: You have to move, missus. Or you'll lose the visit. Go on!

Lila and Martha bundle her towards door. Exit Alice.

LILA: She reminds me of me Granny. She was from Cork. You couldn't understand a word out of her mouth. Though I only met her the once. She was even from the city — Sweet Blackpool she called it, the northside of Cork. I think in them days the city was like the country is now. Me Ma left me with her for a week. I'd a brilliant time. I never saw her again. She's dead now.

MARTHA: We were supposed to be getting a murderer. Not a fucking bogwoman.

LILA: You were very hard on her, Martha.

MARTHA: Yeah well. It's not right is it? Mixing them in with us. They should keep like with like.

LILA: I wonder what she did. She never said.

MARTHA: *(Mimicking)* As a matter of fact I did keep a few sheep. Delo'll hit the roof. *(Rifling in Alice's bag)*

LILA: Ah now leave it out.

MARTHA: She might be a plant. The screws are all culchies.

LILA: A grasser.

MARTHA: Who do they think they are?

LILA: Who do they think we are?

MARTHA: *(Laughing)* Who do they think she is?

Buzzer sounds and door opens. Enter **Delo***.*

MARTHA: Did you see her?

DELO: Who?

MARTHA: She's an oul one.

Delo *goes to* **Alice***'s bunk and opens up her suitcase. Takes up crocheted square of bright colours (in progress) and smells it.*

DELO: Weird. What would you say that is?

MARTHA: Weird.

LILA: It's the smell of turfsmoke.

Delo *continues rummaging in case. Takes out framed photo.*

DELO: Take a look at this. A dog. A fucking dog.

LILA: It's not fair. Leave it.

DELO: The moral high ground.

MARTHA: She's not a murderer in any case.

DELO: The word out there is that she is. A knife woman no less.

LILA: I don't believe it.

DELO: You! Make a cuppa. Martha, give us a hand.

Delo takes the gear from tracksuit bottoms. **Martha** *clears space on table and they begin to make up orders.* **Lila** *makes tea.*

DELO: We're a bit short today so go easy. Err not on the generous side. Harry couldn't get in himself. He sent that pox merchant Freddie Roe instead. Freddie Roe! Harry'll be sorry he crossed me. Wouldn't you think a solicitor'd have more cop. Ira Lip was on visiting duty. Do you know what she said to me? What an actual screw said to me? 'It's hard to get good staff these days.' The fucking dogs in the street could tell Freddie Roe was a skag merchant. Sure he may as well have had 'junkie' tattooed in neon lights across his forehead. And ladies, from this moment on I'll have to review the freebie situation. The in-cell freebie situation. No graft, no gear — that's the motto round here. *(To* **Martha***)* You're alright. But Missy there, well … I'm only a humble trader. I can ill-afford to carry any dead weight. I can't get over that bastard Freddie Roe. He's no idea who he's taking on here. Have you nothing to say for yourself? Cat got your tongue?

LILA: You know I can't go out there.

MARTHA: Lookit, Delo, I don't mind doing her share. Just stop fucking around with her head, will you? She's not able for it.

DELO: You're her counsellor, is that it? But! But! I am not a charity organisation. Pull yourself together, Lila. We know what happens to them that go to pieces. Eh?

LILA: Fuck you and your gear. I'll do without.

DELO: Easy said. Now. Oh we'll see how cocky you are the next time you need your fix. You'd gut your own granny for a hit. You'll be begging for it. You'd lick it off a scabby mickey.

MARTHA: Give over. Give her a break. She's not well. She doesn't eat. She hasn't been out for fresh air since An—... in a long while. Have a bit of pity.

DELO: Pity! Don't make me laugh.

Martha conceals deals about her person and goes to mouthpiece.

MARTHA: Martha Casey requests permission to collect laundry for cell 27.

VOICE: Permission granted.

DELO: Give nothing to Sharon Doyle.

MARTHA: Jesus. Now you tell me. I took an order from her. She's paid and all. Why? What'll I say to her?

DELO: Just say I said no. She's aware of what it's about.

MARTHA: She'll fucken savage me.

DELO: Hazard of the trade m'dear. We'll negotiate a little danger money, eh?

*Buzzer sounds and **Martha** Exits.*

Delo and Lila circling table slowly.

DELO: C'mere to me, you.

LILA: Keep away from me.

DELO: Don't try my patience. 'Fuck you and your gear' quote, unquote.

LILA: Leave it out.

DELO: You've changed your tune.

LILA: I can't take any more.

DELO: *(Stripping off sweatshirt to reveal large tattooed snake on arm)* Tell that to Snakey. Go on. Say it to him!

LILA: You're off your rocker.

DELO: Come to Snakey. Come on. Snakey wants you. Don't you, baby? Ah look Snakey's sad? Has lil Lila hurt his feelings? What's that? Eh? *(Listening to snake)* Lila's a bold girl? Lila should be punished? How so? Oooh. Nasty.

LILA: Stop. I'll ring for help.

DELO: What? What did you say? Did my ears deceive me? You heard the same, Snakey? Lila is a rat. Snakey says Lila is a rat. And what do hungry Snakeys do to rats?

*Pace increases until they are running, dodging around table. **Delo** finally catches up with **Lila** forcing her to her knees gripping her by the hair.*

DELO: Say sorry to Snakey. Go on. Apologise. Say it — I'm sorry.

LILA: No.

***Delo** hits **Lila** across face.*

DELO: Say it.

LILA: No.

***Delo** continues hitting her.*

DELO: Now will you say it?

LILA: No.

***Delo** beats her until —*

DELO: What?

***Lila** makes sound like whimper.*

DELO: Louder!

LILA: Sorr— *(Whimper)*

DELO: Louder. *(Clatter)* Louder. Say it.

LILA: I'm sorry.

DELO: Now we're getting somewhere. *(Lets go of **Lila**)* Kiss Snakey. Do it.

Lila kisses the tattooed snake.

LILA: I'm going to be sick.

Lila retches and runs for the wash-hand basin.

DELO: You're disgusting. Do you hear me? Disgusting. After all I've done for you. Working my fingers to the bone. And for what? Eh? Sleeveen bitch. Isn't she Snakey? Slither in the grass. That's the thanks you get, Snakey. The cushiest cell on the wing. There's young ones out there would give their eye teeth to be in this cell. Do you hear me, wagon?

Lila slumps to floor of cubicle. Crawls out on all fours towards her bunk.

DELO: The state of you. Crawling. You're pathetic. I hope you cleaned up in there after yourself?

LILA: There was nothing to come up. Why are you picking on me? I didn't do anything.

DELO: Precisely! Precisely! You didn't do anything. Isn't that the crux of the matter? She didn't do anything Snakey!

LILA: This has to stop. I can't take any more. You're driving me mad.

DELO: I'm driving you mad? I'm driving her mad, Snakey!

LILA: Mad. Like you drove Annie. She couldn't take anymore. And it'll be me next. Do you see? You won't let me in peace. Picking on me all the time. I never done nothing bad to you. I was only trying to … *(Delo laughs)* to … to … to do me time.

DELO: *(Laughs)* If you can't do the time, don't do the crime.

Silence. Eventually …

DELO: Here, have a cuppa. How about it? Huh? Bygones be and all that.

LILA: No.

DELO: I'll put Snakey away. *(Puts on sweatshirt)* Listen to me Lila. This is all for your own good. Chastisement. Forges character. You don't want to end up a spineless blubber of mush. It hurts me more than it hurts you etcetera etcetera etcetera. You find that strange. Believe me. I'm older and wiser than you. I know my way around this system. You think I like coming the heavy? That I enjoy it? You have to wise up.

Silence.

DELO: Do you remember when you came in here? You were beautiful. Glossy hair. Bright eyes. I thought to myself — Lila there could be a model. Up on the catwalks. Earning a fortune. You were a real good-looker. Then Annie died. By her own hand, let it be said. She chose. A woman's right to choose. That's a motto of mine. Look at you now. You've let yourself go. Big time.

LILA: You tortured her. You wouldn't give her any peace. You were at her morning, noon and night.

DELO: I was at her. Are you jealous? Is that the nub? The crux? Miss Know-it-all. There was stuff between Annie and

me you knew nothing about. Fuck all. Do you understand?
If you were in possession of all the facts you wouldn't be
coming out with this shite. But you're not. In possession. So
don't judge. If you knew what I did for Annie. I'm not one
to blow my own trumpet; but if you only knew what I did
for that girl, you'd be down on your hands and knees
thanking God for putting you in the same spot on the same
planet in the same universe as me. At the same time!

LILA: I saw you with me own eyes.

DELO: Ha. With your own deluded junkie eyes! You saw
nothing.

Silence. Eventually ...

DELO: Here. Have a cuppa. Go on. Or? A little something
to show there's no hard feelings? Eh? Hmmn?

LILA: Tea. Nothing else.

DELO: Ooogh. Brave.

LILA: I'm going to do it. I'm getting off the gear.

DELO: Sure.

LILA: I'm going to get clean and put myself back together.
The doctor'll give me something. Just to help me with the
crash. And tomorrow, or the next day or ... soon in any
case, I'm going to sign up for the school and go everyday.
I'll force myself out. I'll do the yoga. I'll do the cookery
lessons. Nutrition and all they do. And I'll start eating.
Build meself up. I'm really going to get myself together.

DELO: Yeah. Yeah. Yeah. Yeah. I'll tune in tomorrow at
the same time and see what you've to say for yourself then.
Pul-eese Delo, just a little hit to take the edge off. Listen,
I've heard it all before.

They sit at table. **Delo** *pours tea. Buzzer sounds and door opens.*
Enter **Alice**.

DELO: Welcome. Welcome. We were just talking about
you. A nice hot cuppa. You look like you could do with
one. And a biccy.

ALICE: Alice Kane. How are ye? You're Dolores I'd say.
You're very kind. I'll just hoke out my slippers. Do you
know my feet are aching off me?

DELO: Aye. The feet are the most vulnerable part of the
body. A medical doctor told me that. I'm murdered with the
corns myself. Murdered I am.

ALICE: Ach but it's an exhausting business. This doing
nothing. I'd not be a tenth as tired after putting in a long
day in the garden. The standing around and the sitting
around and the waiting. They called me out for to see my
solicitor, the new one. She's very good. She knows her stuff
alright. But sure I only had ten minutes with her and she
had to be off. The rest of the time was hanging about. And
they wouldn't let me back in here for ages.

DELO: *(Picking up* **Alice**'*s inflection)* I was just saying to Lila
here that it'll be nice to have a mature woman in the cell for
a change. Wasn't I, love? Poor Lila's not feeling the best.
Time of month. Your heart'd break for the young ones. It's
not here they should be at all, at all, but getting proper
medical help for their troubles. Drugs most of them. God
love them. Sure isn't it a terrible world out there? Settle
yourself in there.

ALICE: You don't look a bit well, Lila. Is there nothing
you can take for it. I haven't so much as an aspirin on me.

LILA: I'm alright. I'll be okay.

DELO: She's a brave wee thing.

ALICE: I used get them fierce bad myself when I was young. I'd have to take to the bed for the day with the hot jar. My boys were a great help. For there were things that couldn't be left, do you know. The work. Have ye not a hot … water bottle?

LILA: I'm fine.

DELO: Deed'n you're not. You poor creature. Lie out there and have a stretch. All that hunching is bad for you. You'll end up with curvature of the spine.

LILA: As if you care. As if you give two fucks how I feel. She's only codding you, missus.

DELO: Sure what can you expect. God love them. Martha Casey's taking her time.

Silence. Eventually …

DELO: How do you think the elections will go? Of course we've no votes. Us criminals forfeit the right to vote. Did you know that Alice? Disenfranchised. Disgraced. And disgusted. Eh Lila? There's no one running on a general amnesty ticket. That's who I'd vote for. If I had one. Open the prison doors wide. A clean slate. Start from scratch.

ALICE: Sure you have to have prisons. The country's gone to the dogs as it is.

DELO: You wouldn't go a general amnesty?

ALICE: Not only that but I'd build a sight more of them. And put the real crooks in. You'd need a fair-sized county I can tell you. And they're only the ones I know personally.

DELO: Do you tell me so? You must hang out with a fierce bad lot.

ALICE: I'd start with the politicians themselves. I wrote eleven times to the Minister for Justice since … since my arrest. Wrongful arrest. For I was only defending what's mine. And her a woman. And me a widow these ten years. She must have a heart of stone for not so much as a word did I get in reply.

DELO: There's no votes here. Sure and there's not Lila? Lila!

LILA: No.

ALICE: Do you know I voted for the same fellow for all of twenty years and I voted for his father before him. And do you know the last time I was in Carrick I ran into the wife of him and do you know she near jumped out of her skin. Across the street with her like a whippet. She ducked into the Bush — that's a hotel — and all I wanted to find out was if himself was going to be at the clinic that night. I cycled all the way in for that! In the rain. And he wasn't there.

DELO: Are you following this Lila?

ALICE: It was the nephew. Taking the clinic that night. They've no children themselves. I suppose that's cross enough to carry. But the nephew. As if I'd discuss my business with the nephew. A young buck that only did his Leaving last year. Him and his ponytail. I left a note. I haven't heard a titter since. If there'd been a reply it would have been forwarded for Mikey is a very decent man and the events that transpired have never changed in the least his manner towards me.

DELO: Terrible. Do you hear that Lila? So Mikey is?

ALICE: The postman. A great singer. *(Sings)*

> *They're going to tax the crutches and they'll tax the wooden legs,*
> *They're going to tax the bacon, bread and butter, cheese and eggs;*

They're going to tax old pensioners as heavy as they can,
And they'll double tax young girls that go looking for a man

(Hums next two lines then)

They'll tax the ground we walk upon, and the clothes that
keep us warm,
And they're going to tax the childer on the night before
they're born.

Now.

DELO: Now. What did you say?

ALICE: Mikey, I said, would it be a trouble to you to forward any letters ...

DELO: No. No. What did you say to the politician?

ALICE: Very little. As a matter of policy, even at the best of times. Put very little in writing. Ever.

DELO: Are you taking this in Lila?

ALICE: I just asked him as a life long supporter of himself and his father before him to contact me before the case came to court. I was out on bail at the time and do you know I had to cycle in to the town every single day to sign on at the Garda station, like a common criminal. It wasn't that he wouldn't know the ins and the outs. Sure the dogs in the street knew the ins and the outs of it.

DELO: Dogs in the street, Lila!

ALICE: Not a peep out of him. It's only when you hit rock bottom that you know who your friends are. I could count them on one hand. For as long as I live I'll not cast a vote for him, his seed or his breed or his party again.

DELO: You must be intending to get out of here so.

ALICE: It's only a matter of time. *(She laughs)* And I've a sight of that.

DELO: *(To Lila)* If she doesn't come back soon, you're going to have to go out and look for her. So, Alice, how long are you in for?

ALICE: Life.

DELO: That could be anything.

ALICE: I'm appealing it.

DELO: Good luck to you Missus.

*Lila, who has been growing more distressed throughout, retches and rushes for the cubicle. She pulls curtain and sounds of retching can be heard inside. **Alice** hovers outside cubicle.*

DELO: Remember. Plastic bag!

ALICE: That child needs a doctor.

DELO: Wasn't I only saying the same thing to her myself. But the young now. Would they listen?.

ALICE: It's pitiful to hear it. Is there nothing to be done?

DELO: God 'elps them wot 'elp themselves. Have you childer yourself?

ALICE: Two boys. Grand boys and very good to me. Off in America oh near fifteen years, the oldest lad. The younger fellow near enough the same. The first one went and sent the fare. Isn't that the way? They work very hard. But as soon as they can they'll be over. As soon as they can get away. I always fancied I'd love a daughter. But it wasn't to be. *(At cubicle)* Lila, are you alright, child?

DELO: *(Moving to cubicle)* Pore wee thang. Lila. Oh Lila. Can we get you anything dear?

LILA: You fuck off.

DELO: Isn't that lovely talk? She's not like this when she's well. Don't think ill of her. We all say things we regret when we're under the weather. It's alright Lila. We understand dear.

LILA: Fuck off you. *(Retches)*

ALICE: Have you children yourself?

DELO: I've four meself. Two of each. My mother is rearing the two youngest. John and Shane. The girls … they're away. Yes. Like yours. Off to find fame and fortune in the wide wide world. You know what kids are these days. They write. Yes. Very regular, a letter or a card. A lovely postcard of the Eiffel Tower only the other day. Paris. When they were living here they never missed a visit. I have to hand it to them. Never a minute's trouble. Oh a credit to me they are. Not like some of the scumbags you meet in here.

ALICE: All you can do is give them the start in life. What they turn out like is a mystery for there're them that has love and care by the bucket who go to the bad, and there're them that are treated worst than dogs that shine through in goodness in the fullness of time. Isn't it the queer thing?

Lila comes out very unsteadily and goes to chair. Alice goes to get her tea, but Delo in a proprietorial fashion muscles in.

DELO: Here pet, let me. Listen Lila. Have you any idea what's keeping Martha? Will you listen to me now. Lila? Lila?

ALICE: She's all confused. Dehydration is a terrible thing altogether. It can fuddle up your mind a sight.

DELO: She should be back way before now. You'd not know what'd be going on out there. Jesus. I'm going to have to go and suss it out.

ALICE: Aren't we entitled to see a doctor?

DELO: Oh yes, Alice. A constitutional right no doubt.

Delo goes to mouthpiece.

DELO: Dolores Roche from cell 27 requests permission to collect laundry.

VOICE: Someone from cell 27 already signed out to collect laundry. Permission refused.

DELO: She's a crucifix up her hole that one. Excuse me Alice.

ALICE: Will you not get her a doctor?

DELO: Dolores Roche requests permission to use recreation yard for thirty minutes. Please.

VOICE: Permission granted.

DELO: *(To Lila)* Lookit, I won't be long. Do you want something before I go?

ALICE: Isn't it plain she needs a doctor?

DELO: *(Laughs)* She needs her head examined.

Buzzer sounds and door opens.

DELO: I'm out of here.

Exit Delo. Alice goes to Lila and examines her, feels her forehead, and her throat glands.

ALICE: You're all shivery. Would it be glandular fever? You have a terrible clammy feel about your skin.

LILA: She's gone.

ALICE: She is surely. And good riddance, if you ask me.

Alice gets cardigan and wraps it around **Lila**.

LILA: She's a monster.

ALICE: There's something not right there.

LILA: You've no idea.

ALICE: It's in her eyes. The look you'd get in a dog that goes prowling lambs at night.

LILA: I'm afraid.

Alice goes to mouthpiece.

ALICE: Hello. Hello. Are ye hearing me?

Squawk.

ALICE: Holy Mother.

VOICE: Yes?

ALICE: Hello? Are you there?

VOICE: Please state your name and your request.

ALICE: It's a doctor I'm after. This is Alice Kane. From County Leitrim. I need a doctor for young Lila here.

VOICE: The doctor is available between 8.00 and 8.45 in the morning.

ALICE: That's no use to us. Can ye not call one out?

VOICE: The doctor is available between 8.00 and 8.45 in the morning.

ALICE: Yes. Yes. I heard ye. It's not good enough. This girl is very sick.

LILA: Please, Alice, leave it. I don't want to see anyone.

ALICE: Hello? Are ye there?

VOICE: Please state the nature of the request.

ALICE: Amn't I after telling … hello … hello? Hello? It's gone dead on me.

LILA: It'll only make trouble. She'll kill me.

ALICE: Deedn't she won't, daughter.

LILA: You don't know her. She killed Annie. As good as killed her. Annie who was in your bunk there before you. She drove her to kill herself. It's the same as if she'd stabbed her with a knife through the heart. Oh I'm sorry, I didn't mean to … I wasn't …

ALICE: So you heard all about it?

LILA: Just that you'd killed your fellah. Though we thought it was a mistake when we seen you. You don't look a bit like a murderer.

ALICE: And I'm not, for it was a pure act of self-defence. And it wasn't my fellah I killed. *(Laughs)* The idea of it. Shamy McGrane'd turn the strongest stomach. And I'm not sorry I did it. For I'd have no peace for the rest of my days.

LILA: What happened?

ALICE: Shamy started sniffing round soon after my own husband died. And what was he after? A few poor rushy acres? Christ knows. And look where it got him! The greed of that man. He'd already got thirty acres off us. A few here and there over the years. It all adds up. When Paddy — that's my husband — died, he thought he was onto a good thing. For ten years he had me plagued. Breaking fences. Letting his cows into my garden. Poisoning the well, would you believe? He'd stoop to anything. And worse he got. He took to turning up at the house in the dead of night. Addled he'd be, on the loony juice he got up in Arigna. This night in anyway I must have left the latch off the door for even

with the barks out of Mac by the time I got full waking he
was standing in the kitchen and he with a big head of drink
on him. Mac, the poor creature, was lying whimpering in
the corner, blood coming out of the side of his wee mouth.
He was the best dog. Shamy must have landed a boot on
him. He made a run at me and round the table in the middle
of the kitchen we went for what seemed like hours. Now
you have to picture Shamy — the girth of a hay-barn he was
and the hands on him like lump hammers. I was standing
by the drawer of the table and my hand went in and found
the big knife. And ...

LILA: And?

ALICE: Well I've not a great recollection of the events
after. I know the dawn came up and I was outside burying
poor Mac in the orchard. Beside the back wall. Shamy was
lying stone dead on the kitchen floor. I'm not sure how I
did it or where I got the strength from.

Silence. Eventually ...

ALICE: I thought I'd bury Shamy too. But there was no
moving him and there was blood everywhere. Up the walls
even. And I was covered in it. So. I just waited. I washed
myself, and put on fresh clothes and I made a cup of tea. I
sat out in the garden. Do you know it was a beautiful day
and I never felt such an intense happiness as I felt sitting
there in the garden. Do you have a garden?

LILA: I live in the flats. I mean I used to.

ALICE: I think I've loved my garden more than any
human. Even my sons. Isn't that a strange thing? That
dawn ... the bees were only just coming out. At the borage.
And you could nearly see the pea flowers opening. And
there were tiny courgettes, only about a finger long. And I
went about taking great handfuls of herbs and breathing
them deep into me. I remember thinking wasn't it just the

way with life, for I'd finally got on top of the weeding the day before and I'd promised myself that I'd keep on top of it. Then Mikey came with the post — it was only an ESB bill — and all was revealed.

Lila is calmed almost to sleep by the story.

ALICE: *(Singing/humming)*

> You are like the swan that sails on the ocean
> And making motion with both its wings
> Your snowy breast would be a potion
> For any Lord or an Irish King
> For you are youthful, fair and handsome
> And here no longer can I stay
> What can t be cured must be endured
> So farewell darling I must away.

ALICE: You're a wee bit better. Can I get you something?

LILA: It comes in waves.

VOICE: Alice Kane, please. Alice Kane.

Alice goes to mouthpiece.

ALICE: Yes? Hello? It's me.

VOICE: Permission granted for recreation period of thirty minutes. Door will open in ten seconds.

ALICE: But it was a doctor I was looking for. I don't understand. Hello?

LILA: Take it. Go to one of the warders. Tell her *you re* sick. Don't bring them to the cell. If Delo finds out …

ALICE: Hush daughter and don't be getting yourself all tangled.

*Buzzer sounds and door opens. Exit **Alice**. **Lila** holds herself and rocks catatonically.*

LILA: O God. I don't feel good. Help me. O Christ. Help me. No. No I won't. Jesus. *(She begins to whimper as she rocks. Eventually goes to mouthpiece)* I can't. I can't …

VOICE: Please state your name and the nature of your request.

LILA: O God.

VOICE: Please state your name and the nature of your request.

*Lila in state of desperation and agitation goes to **Delo**'s bunk and hauls herself up onto it. She roots in **Delo**'s stash till she finds a box of pills. She has trouble getting them open. Wraps duvet around her. Looking out window takes pills one by one.*

LILA: Lovely roundy moon, check. Weeping willow, check. Leaves falling, check. Yellow, check. Top of the lamppost, check. Election poster, check. Your woman on it, check. Truck carrying bricks for the new prison, check. One crane, check. The other crane, check. Weeds on the wall, check. Man hurrying past, check. Glittery black roof, check. Clouds, check. Black clouds away over the canal, check. Dark blue clouds too, check. Rain, check. Rain, check. All the lovely rain …

Lila slumps down on bunk and pulls duvet completely over herself. Rain getting up outside, finally reaching torrential levels, and sound of wind howling far off. Buzzer sounds and door opens.

*Enter **Martha**. She is spaced out and soaked through. She clocks figure asleep in bunk.*

MARTHA: *(Softly)* Del? Thank God for small mercies. Lila? Lila? *(Checking cubicle)* Wonders will never fucking cease. What came over her? That's brilliant.

She goes to table and begins sorting scrunched up bits of paper money from different pockets, smoothing them out. She counts the *pile three times. She's still short. She goes to her bunk and gets a fiver from inside the pillowcase. Adds it to pile. She's still short. Goes to **Lila**'s bunk and then locker and is rummaging quietly looking for money when ... Buzzer sounds. Door opens. Enter **Alice**, also soaked.*

MARTHA: Fuck.

ALICE: *(Towelling herself)* You should dry yourself off before you get your death.

MARTHA: Sh. For fuck sake will you keep it down. The dragon sleeps. She'll be on my back for sure. Where's agriphonic?

ALICE: What?

MARTHA: Lila. Did she go out with you?

ALICE: I got some aspro's for her.

MARTHA: Sh. Fuckit. She loves her nap does our Delo. I'm in deep shit when she gets up. I'd a fucking brilliant time. Me cousin is in. Mags. A total loop the looper. Great crack. Sh.

ALICE: I don't understand.

MARTHA: She just got in this morning. Two year she got. Mags'd be me first cousin. Her Ma is me aunt. D'ye see? She's the image of me. The spit. Except she has mad hair. All frizzed out. You'd think she was after sticking her hand in an electric socket. You'd love our Mags, Alice. Whoops.

ALICE: No. Lila. They might have got her a doctor.

MARTHA: Will you keep it down.

*Buzzer sounds and door opens. Enter **Delo**.*

DELO: What the fuck is going on? You! What happened?

MARTHA: *(Acting straighter then she is)* It's cool, Delo. Jayz I thought you were having a nap.

Delo goes to bunk and pulls back duvet.

DELO: My eyes better be deceiving me. Hey! Come on.

ALICE: She isn't a bit well, that girl. Gently with her!

MARTHA: She's in deep shit now.

DELO: Here. Christ. She's fast aslee— Christ. *(Backing off)*

ALICE: Let her rest. What is it? *(Going to bunk)* Lila? Lila! Oh merciful Mother, let it not be. *(She climbs up on bunk)* Come on girl. Answer me. Lila. *(Puts her ear to her chest. Feels her jugular)* Get some help! *(Slapping her about face)* Come on love. Now. Lila. Lila. Get on that thing, quick.

Martha goes to mouthpiece.

DELO: Don't you dare. Get away from that.

ALICE: We're losing her. Get some help, woman.

DELO: Get her down from there.

Delo manhandles Lila down from bunk to floor. Starts shaking her.

DELO: Wake up. Do you hear? Wake up.

MARTHA: O God. What's wrong with her? O God.

DELO: Get a grip. There's nothing wrong with her. She's putting it on. *(Shaking Lila violently)*

ALICE: *(Pulling Delo off)* You'll hurt her. *(To Martha)* Get on that yoke!

DELO: *(Laughing)* Hurt! Wake up? Do you hear? Lila! Get the fuck up!

Delo and Alice tussle for control of body.

ALICE: *(Examining Lila gently)* I think we're losing her. *(To Martha)* Martha, will you get some help? Child! For God's sake.

DELO: If you lay so much as a finger on that door ... get away from it!

MARTHA: This isn't happening. This definitely isn't happening.

ALICE: *(Trying to revive her)* Martha please. Get help.

DELO: Do nothing Martha. She's only putting it on.

Alice smoothes back Lila's hair and composes her limbs. She tucks the duvet around her.

ALICE: We've lost her.

MARTHA: No. No. No. Oh God.

DELO: We're up the bleeding Sewanee now. Fuck it. They'll turn this place over.

MARTHA: *(Moaning and rocking)* Oh God. Mammy. Mammy. Oh God. Oh God.

Delo goes to her bunk and takes stuff from mattress and begins searching for hiding place.

DELO: Give us a hand Mar. Martha! Get a grip. We've got to get rid of this.

Martha doesn't move. Delo puts gear under Lila's pillow.

DELO: Alice Kane, you've seen nothing. Do you hear me? Do you? I'll have the tongue out of your head if you breathe a word. Do you get it? Me drift?

ALICE: The poor child. The poor child.

Blackout.

END PART ONE

Part Two

*The cell, one month later, November, full moon. Another month
crossed off on* **Martha**'s *chart.* **Alice**'s *bunk is now adorned with
portrait of dog and two posters — one of a forest glade and the
other of a country landscape covered in snow, a small cottage with
smoke from the chimney visible. She too has a chart with one
month marked off. What was* **Lila**'s *bunk is now stripped of all
personal effects and has an institutional look about it.*

Afternoon and strong light streams in through window. **Martha**
and **Alice** *at table, both crocheting,* **Alice** *working on large
square;* **Martha** *working on small somewhat lopsided piece. It is
very cold.* **Alice** *wears fingerless mittens and is well muffled up. In
contrast* **Martha** *is in short sleeved T-shirt.*

MARTHA: I'm never going to get the hang of this. It looks
stupid. Why won't it sit straight?

ALICE: The tension.

MARTHA: Huh? Tension? I'm a bit tense?

ALICE: No. No. Some stitches you're doing tight and
some stitches you're doing loose. You should aim for all
stitches of a regular tension.

MARTHA: I don't have the patience for it.

ALICE: *(Measuring her quilt against her bunk)* I'm nearly
there. Then we'll get going on yours. All you need is
practice.

MARTHA: I need a new set of hands.

ALICE: You've your fingers a bit raw.

MARTHA: Me nerves.

ALICE: You're doing great …

MARTHA: I wish. I'd love a bath. It's great when you're coming off gear. A long soak.

ALICE: With bubbles. I bet you therc'll be baths in the new prison. I heard the toilets flush by themselves, every three minutes.

MARTHA: Would that be at night as well? Will we be in by Christmas?

ALICE: I heard that it'll be March before we're moved. I heard there's two to a cell and all self-contained. Stainless steel everywhere. Your own shower in the cell itself. And blue curtains.

MARTHA: We'll do our own cooking and all.

ALICE: They'd not give us knives, daughter. Would they?

MARTHA: It was still only a building site the day they buried Lila. God. Hard to believe she's a month dead. I dreamt about her again. It's freezing. *(Putting on jumper)* I was boiling a minute ago.

ALICE: Christ mind her. The poor child.

MARTHA: 'It's cold here. And lonely. Help me.' That's what she said. She was there in front of me large as life. She was Alice. I swear. Seriously. If I'd of reached out I'd of touched her. She was plain as day.

ALICE: It'd be natural you'd dream of Lila, daughter. That's how they keep in touch.

MARTHA: What?

ALICE: The dead. It's their way of talking to us.

MARTHA: Jesus. You're giving me the willies.

ALICE: She might have unfinished business. Something she wants you to do for her. Or something she wants to tell

you. Some warning. Or maybe something she meant to say
to you when she was alive.

MARTHA: Stop it. It's hard enough dealing with the
living.

ALICE: Next time you dream of her ask her outright.
'What can I do for you Lila?' You'll see then.

MARTHA: What?

ALICE: What what?

MARTHA: What'll I see?

ALICE: Where? What?

MARTHA: Forget it, right.

Silence.

ALICE: I dreamt about my sister Katy for months after she
died. The one dream always — I'd be digging at the end of
her garden under this old ash tree. The same spot every
time. So I got the spade and off I went up to Katy's house
— her son Gerry of course had it after she died. Glic that
one. I waited till he was off in Lanzarote with Siobhán and
the children. I went up there in the dead of night but there
was a full moon so it was no problem to me to see what I
was doing. I thought I'd find money or deeds to land
maybe. I even had a mad notion that I'd find jewels. I was
young do you see. Katy was a fair bit older than me.

MARTHA: Did you find anything?

ALICE: Oh aye. I did rightly.

MARTHA: Come on, Alice.

ALICE: A little skeleton. A handful really. A wee baby
buried.

MARTHA: What did you do?

ALICE: Do? Do? I left it of course. Exactly where I found it. You'd not know the land had been disturbed at all, at all.

MARTHA: But surely Kate ... Katy ... wanted you to do something.

ALICE: I think she just wanted me to know. Katy went fierce religious towards the end. I had a few masses said. Special intentions. And never had the dream again after.

MARTHA: When Lila died, I thought Delo was so understanding. She just kept me stoned off me face for the month.

ALICE: Shush now. You're getting there.

MARTHA: Yeah! Sixty hours, fifteen minutes and forty six seconds.

ALICE: You're a dinger for keeping track of time.

MARTHA: I'm sweating again. Buckets.

ALICE: Keep that geansaí on. You're asking for a chill.

MARTHA: I wouldn't be going full blown, would I Alice? Is there a funny smell off my sweat? Smell it.

ALICE: No. No. Of course not. Your body's only trying to come back to itself. You said it yourself, Martha. It's ironing out the kinks. Another few weeks and you won't know yourself. It has to find its way in the world all over again. It's like you've just been born.

MARTHA: It's like me body's not me own any more. Do you know what I mean? Like it does things by itself. You wouldn't know what to expect. Out of the blue. The diarrhoea ... it felt like I shat a mountain yesterday. There is nothing left inside me. My feet were totally numb all last night.

ALICE: You're doing great.

MARTHA: Am I Alice? Am I? I do be thinking about the virus all the time now. Maybe that's why I'm this sick? I've come off gear before and I don't remember it being this bad. The virus is right in your cells — invisible. Working away quietly. All the time. I'm not supposed to get stressed out.

ALICE: I think you're a very brave young woman.

MARTHA: I'm very fucken stressed.

Martha bends double with cramps.

MARTHA: Oh Jesus. Breathe slowly out. Breathe slowly in. Breathe slowly out. I bet you Delo has a ju-ju doll somewhere with pins stuck in it. And it has my face on it.

ALICE: That one woman should strike such fear into us! We'd be much better off on our own, do you know. In fact it could be pleasant enough here.

MARTHA: It'd be great to be rid of her alright but … unless we escape.

ALICE: Aye. And pigs might fly. You can't escape yourself, daughter. Isn't that the truth?

Silence.

MARTHA: I was thinking that if I keep it together, if I stay straight, I could maybe ask to see Jasmine on a visit. What do you think?

ALICE: Jasmine. Have you ever smelt it? Beautiful. Beautiful. I tried to grow it once but too much frost. The name itself brings back the smell. Jasmine.

MARTHA: We used go for a nap every afternoon. I wouldn't draw the curtains. We'd sleep in the sun. A hot smell. Milky. On the big settee. She'd have her thumb in her mouth and she'd get a hold of me hair, and twiddle it around her finger. I had loads of bald patches from her. But I didn't mind. Maybe she's forgotten who I am?

ALICE: You never forget your own.

MARTHA: She still thinks I'm in England. Working. I do be afraid the other kids in the flats would say something. Kids can be awful cruel. You tell one lie and before you know where you are you're up to your oxters in it.

ALICE: I know.

MARTHA: His Ma is very good to her but. Maybe when I get out, myself and Jasmine could come and stay on your farm. For a visit.

ALICE: Well farm is stretching it a bit.

Martha cramps again, bends double, then sits rocking on chair.

MARTHA: It's like I ate glass. Something's ripping me apart inside.

ALICE: Would you not see the doctor in the morning?

MARTHA: That pox merchant! I'd rather die. The last time I saw him was when he told me I had the virus. I went in and he said, 'I've your results here. You're positive.' 'What?' I says. I didn't know what he was talking about. I thought I'd just done an ordinary blood test — for anaemia. The same with the other girls. We didn't know you see. We'd no idea. He's a filthy bastard. He gives you an internal even if you go in with a cold in your nose. A chance to grope. Bastards. Doctors and cops and priests and fucking teachers. All fucking bastards. I hate them. I swear Alice I hate them.

*Buzzer sounds. Door opens and enter **Delo** in a rage calling behind her —*

DELO: Yis gee bags. A pox on yis're diddies.

MARTHA: What happened?

DELO: You'd love to know.

Silence.

DELO: Mother Macree and … and the Zombie from the Night of the Living Dead. You look like shite Martha Casey.

Silence.

DELO: *(To **Martha** on chair)* Up.

ALICE: She's bad with the cramps. Leave her rest. Take mine.

DELO: She has you fooled and all. Looking for attention that's what it is.

ALICE: Have pity woman.

DELO: *(Goes to sit, then notices something on her locker)* I didn't leave that box there. It was on the other side of the Chanel. Who moved it? Eh? Fucking typical. You can't have anything in this kip.

Delo *takes **Alice**'s chair. **Alice** goes and sits on her bunk.*

DELO: Yis are as thick as thieves. Martha's a certified thief. Not a very good one. What was it Mar? A pair of Levi's?

MARTHA: It was sixty.

DELO: Six?

MARTHA: Sixty pairs.

DELO: Oh excuse me. Four years for sixty pairs of Levi's. Pathetic really. Of course Alice, you now are the real thing. The genuine article. We're only in the halfpenny place. Aren't we Martha?

MARTHA: No.

DELO: No? Where are we then?

MARTHA: Give us a break.

DELO: I gave you plenty of them. What thanks did I get? Snake in the grass. The minute me back was turned. We had a good system, you and me. We had the best. Till fuckface put in an appearance. You queered our pitch rightly Alice Kane. Look at the state of her. It's like a fucking nunnery in here. An enclosed bleeding order and the novice won't leave the cell. *(Looking at **Martha**'s piece)* Jesus Martha — what are you hoping to catch with that?

ALICE: She's doing grand.

DELO: You give a whole new meaning to the term needle exchange, Alice Kane.

*Delo has a go at working **Martha**'s piece.*

DELO: This brings me back. Bri-nylon wool. Did you ever hear of bri-nylon wool, Alice. You'd of been too young, Martha. It was all the rage when I was a girl. Miss Shannon in the Central Model School. She taught me to knit. Didn't know I could knit, Alice? Eh? Oh yeah. I spent three years turning the heel of a sock. Four steel needles and bri-nylon wool. Yellow. When I started. You couldn't tell what colour it was by the time I turned that heel. One sock. If only I'd known a one-footed child. Yis are very quiet.

Silence.

DELO: I think it's the best thing that happened in this cell, young Martha there coming clean. And I can assure you all, hand on heart, of my un- un- wavering, yes, that's the word, unwavering support. In any way, on any day, say but the word, and Delo will do her utmost.

MARTHA: Don't be slagging me.

DELO: I got it wrong. I admit it. Umble pie. Give it to me. I'll eat it.

ALICE: Well thank God.

MARTHA: She's messing with our heads.

DELO: All joking aside. We should tackle this together as a community. Community action against drugs. I'm deadly serious, girls. You Martha. The breathing. Excellent. Take a breath, hold it, let it go. Take a breath, hold it. Let it go. God's sweet air, pure and unsullied into your lungs. Sure I'll do it with you. All the exercises. Before you know it you'll be able to go out again. We'll start into the yoga classes. We'll all start. You too Alice. Writing workshops, aromatherapy. Sure we won't know ourselves we'll be that personally developed. Agoraphobia will be a dim and shady memory from the bad times. You'll be the old Martha again. Things will be only fucking brilliant around here.

ALICE: Yes. Yes.

MARTHA: She's codding you missus. You must think we're gobshites. I didn't see you sitting up all night last night and the night before when I was crashing off the gear. I didn't see you washing out me pyjamas when they were drenched with the sweat. Or cleaning me up when I vomited all over myself. Nearly three days I've spent puking me ring up and all you can do is give out about the smell.

DELO: Fair enough. You know what I'm like. Alice is better at that sort of thing. Country folk usually are. They understand these things. Now a cosmopolite like me …

MARTHA: Speak bleeding English, why don't you?

DELO: I love it! I love it! That's the spirit. That'll get you through. And we're right here behind you. Support. That's what you need. Massive amounts of support.

MARTHA: Oh, I don't know. You have me brain scrambled.

DELO: Do you remember Mary Eggs?

MARTHA: I haven't thought of her in years.

DELO: *Mary Eggs. Mary Eggs.*

MARTHA: 'Do you want yer eggs scrambled young one. I'll boil up yer ovaries for you. Little gees. Yis think yis are it with yer little gees.' *(Laughing)* Do you remember the way she'd follow you round trying to grab a hold of you. She'd pull down yer knickers and spit on yer arse. She was a madwoman.

DELO: *(Chanting) Mary Eggs, Mary Eggs, Hairy Eggs and Bacon.*

MARTHA: Mary Eggs wasn't her real name.

DELO: No. But I never heard her called anything else. She was only interested in little girls.

MARTHA: She used scare me shitless. *(Laughing and dancing around) Mary Eggs. Mary Eggs. Hairy Eggs and Bacon. Mary Eggs ...*

DELO: *(Over Martha singing)* The good old days, Alice.

VOICE: Solicitor to see Alice Kane. Alice Kane.

Door buzzer sounds. Door opens.

ALICE: *(In a flap)* Will you be alright? I don't want to leave you ...

MARTHA: Take your visit. Go on. It might be good news.

DELO: We'll play a hand when you come back. You owe me 12 matches, Alice. Virtual matches. Martha, you owe me 2,463. Only joking. Haven't been too hot on the concentration this last while though, have we?

*Exit **Alice**.*

Silence.

DELO: You'd want to watch that one.

Silence.

DELO: You would. I'm telling you. There's more to her nibs than meets the eye.

MARTHA: She's been very good to me.

DELO: Why?

MARTHA: What?

DELO: What's in it for her?

MARTHA: Not everyone is like you Delo Roche.

DELO: Sau-cy. I'm saying nothing. Who was the last person to see Lila alive? Hmm? What do we know about her, really, hmm. Ever tried to ask her about what she did to land in here, hmm? You get a heap of bollickolatry about her innocence. You ask her. Go on. Either she had a lousy legal team or it wasn't self-defence. The word on her is that she's a psychopath.

MARTHA: Leave me alone.

DELO: Think about it.

Silence.

DELO: I'd be the happiest woman alive to see you get yourself together. It would make my day. There is absolutely no reason why we couldn't work together again. The straighter you are the more efficient the business. Since the whole Lila thing — they're watching me the whole time. It makes it very difficult if I'm operating solo. No. No. Think about it. You come back and work for me and I'll pay you strictly in cash. No more gear. Straight money eh? A nice nest egg when you get out. Back to your little Jasmine. It won't be long now. You could take her on a holiday. Somewhere continental. Sun, sea. Sex. I'd say you'd be mad for it by then. The mickey? Are you? Mad for it?

MARTHA: Do you want a cup of tea?

DELO: Does the Pope wear a funny dress?

Delo takes naggin of vodka from under her mattress.

DELO: A little pick me up. *(Doctoring tea)* You'll never guess where I got it.

MARTHA: Where?

DELO: Mags. Mags Mac. Yer cuz. Lovely girl. She was just saying she'd really like to move in with us. A bit of crack alright is your Mags. But … Mother Macree. There's no way she's moving in with Mother Macree. Pity.

MARTHA: Mags and me used go dipping out the airport. You know the signs they have. Beware of pickpockets. What's the first thing you do if you see that sign. Right. Exactly. *(She pats pocket as if to check wallet)* We were cleaning up. Do you really think she'd be able to move in here? That'd be the business.

ALICE: I'm getting on very well these days with Prison Officer O'Reilly. I'm so to speak cultivating the relationship. A few tokens of the esteem in which I hold her

are deeply appreciated. I'd say it won't be long till a polite
request for a little reorganisation will fall on fertile ground.
What would you think of that?

MARTHA: Mags … I don't know.

DELO: She's worried sick about you. You're not yourself.
Not your usual sunny disposition at all, at all. Mags blames
Mother Macree. I'm inclined to agree. And now this lurking
around the cell. Day in, day out. Tut, tut. That's how it
started with Lila. Remember? She wouldn't cross the
threshold. Went into herself. Christ knows we did our best
to help her.

MARTHA: I had a dream about Lila.

DELO: God be good to Lila Byrne, she was a wizard with
the corns.

MARTHA: I can't think straight. I feel really weird.

DELO: Why wouldn't you? *(Climbing up and looking out
window)* That moon, it'd blind you. Like someone turned on
a big lamp in the sky. No wonder it's so nervy around here.
The whole gaff is pre-menstrual. We're all on the one cycle.
Or tending towards that state. Leave a gang of women
together long enough and they'll all end up on the same
cycle. Jaysus it's bitter. Bitter. We won't feel it till
Christmas. *(Takes her hand)* I'll be straight with you. The last
month has been the hardest of all me time. Fuck it, Mar.
I'm lonely. I come back in the cell after slogging me guts out
and all I get is the cold shoulder. I miss Lila too. I loved that
young one, Martha.

MARTHA: Yeah. Yeah. Yeah.

DELO: You think I'm a heartless old wagon …

MARTHA: Spare us …

DELO: No. Hear me out. I *did* love that young one. We were like a family. Who have I? Eh? Answer me that? Who have I? Me boys? They wouldn't know me from Adam. We only had each other. We only *have* each other.

MARTHA: What about you and your girls …

DELO: Do you not get it? None of us has anyone. This is it. Now.

MARTHA: You told Alice your girls were alive … the last letter from Angela, hmm? Do you think Alice believes any of it?

DELO: Martha Casey you're very hard on me. She was blowing off about her sons … she thinks her shit doesn't smell.

MARTHA: *(Pretending to be reading letter)* Doing a strong line with Pierre, the computer expert, wasn't it? And the other one, Marilyn, … Costa Del Poxo, isn't that where she is? Mar dhea! Running, running mind you, a karaoke bar. The Wild One! Wasn't that it? Oh yes Alice … got up to sing on her holliers and next you know she's senior fucking management … Sergio, or was it Georgio, some-bleeding-o. So sorry dearest Ma to think of you rotting in that festering hole. Here's a million pesetas to buy a bit of baccy.

DELO: Have you any idea how much I've spent on *you* over the last month. Eh? Since Lila shuffled off the mortal? Eh? Add it up. Go on! A small fucking fortune.

MARTHA: It suited you to keep me zonkoed. It wasn't for the good of your health. You're a bleedin nympho.

DELO: Are you stupid or are you just pretending to be?

MARTHA: I think you need your head examined.

DELO: Martha my dear, we could be very happy together. If turnip nose was gone, eh? We'd some great times before.

(Sings) Martha my dear, when you find yourself in the thick of it,
help yourself to a bit of what is all around you, pretty girl ...

MARTHA: Had we? Great times?

DELO: Let me give you a little something to ease the pain.
You're very jumpy.

MARTHA: I don't want anything.

DELO: You're unique so.

MARTHA: I'm doing me best to stay off of it.

DELO: Admirable. We'll put you up for canonisation. St.
Martha of the Fallen Angels.

MARTHA: I'm going to keep it together.

DELO: Sure you are. Lookit fuckface will be back any
minute. Is there no chance you'd go out for me today? Me
feet are killing me. I'm a laughing stock out there. Do you
know what Rachel Smith said to me? 'I hear Martha
Casey's after leaving you for the culchie.' I mean to say,
Martha. That's the pits. Go on out for us. Will you?
Straight up money? No strings attached? *(Laughs)* Do you
get it? Do you not get it? Strings?

MARTHA: I'm sick.

DELO: You could be a big help to me. Take the heat off
me. Sure I can't fucking move out there anymore.

MARTHA: I feel weird.

DELO: Jaysus.

MARTHA: I had a dream about Lila.

DELO: For God's sake.

MARTHA: She said I was to do something for her. A message. She had a message for you.

DELO: Will you get a grip? That was the last full moon. Look where that got us. Do you hear me? Do you hear what I'm saying to you? Just don't start. Lunatic! Lunacy! The moon. There's a connection. You just don't get it.

DELO: *(Secreting deals about her person)* I'll leave a little something here for you. *(Leaving tiny ornate box on table)* You see, I do care. Really. Go on. It's a present.

MARTHA: *(Looking)* Pills. I don't want anything.

DELO: They're good. They'll chill you out.

MARTHA: I've never come across them.

DELO: These're not your usual shite. They're tailor made for come-downs. Takes the edge off. And strictly non-addictive. Why, if you went to a doctor private that's probably what you'd be given. They're what all the rich fuckers get from the doc when they're coming off coke. Give your body a chance to get back to normal. Straight up, Martha. On me sons' life. Look, I'll leave them here. And definitely no strings attached.

MARTHA: I want to do it on my own.

DELO: Of course. No sweat. It's just a way of handling it.

Martha takes up pills, examines them.

MARTHA: You're sure these are OK?

DELO: The best. They're official. They'll straighten you out.

Martha leaves pills back in box on table.

MARTHA: Naw. I'm alright thanks.

DELO: It's cool. *(Taking back pills and pocketing them)* I'll just leave one here if you need it.

Delo puts one pill on table.

VOICE: Recreation period for Dolores Roche. Dolores Roche. Recreation period.

Buzzer sounds. Door opens.

DELO: Prison Officer O'Reilly I love you! I really do!

MARTHA: Hang on. What's happening?

DELO: Later babee!

Exit Delo.

Martha alone. She begins to shiver. Rubs her arms to get circulation going. Then starts cleaning up around cell.

MARTHA: Later babee my arse. Who does she think she is? She must think we came down in the last shower. *She'll* give *me* support. Fuck her. And fuck Rachel Smith. It'll be all over the flats by now that I'm with the culchie. Mags would never believe that. Imagine. That's mad. — *(Laughs. Of pill)* It must be the genuine article. His Ma was on stuff like this ... same colour in any case. I might get a night's kip at least. I'm totally wrecked. If I don't get eight hours I'll crack up. I'll start talking to myself. Do you hear me? Jaysus I need to sleep. That's what has me all nervy. Not the moon *(Laughs)* Will you listen! *(Tidying, sings) Mary Eggs, Mary Eggs, Mary Eggs and Bacon.* She had hairs growing out of her nose. I remember that. I'm starting to relax already. *(Holds out hand)* Look at that. Rock steady. Very good. *(Takes pill)*

Martha begins grooming herself, humming. Into cubicle to wash her teeth.

Buzzer sounds. Enter **Alice** *carrying pile of laundry neatly folded. Distracted.*

MARTHA: I'll give you a hand in a minute.

Silence. **Martha** *comes out of cubicle —*

MARTHA: What did she say?

ALICE: Jesus daughter, that solicitor's no use. Her and her briefcase. I should have known better than to have a solicitor from Edgeworthstown. The land of the Quick and the Dead. She couldn't get the figs out of the figs rolls. *(Pause)* There's a delay. With the appeal. That was my news.

MARTHA: There's a jinx on this cell, Alice. I know it. Annie. Then Lila. Who's next? Me. Isn't it?

ALICE: Now child. It's coming up to Christmas. It's a very sad time for all of us. We're all mothers. My sons gone from me. Your Jasmine away from you. All the lost children. There's enough grief in this prison to drown the whole city.

Buzzer sounds. Enter **Delo.**

DELO: *(Taking drink from naggin of vodka)* A hard day at the office. Fancy a little something, Delo? A little pick me up, Delo? A wee tonic, Delo? Soothe the savage beast? Don't mind if I do. Thanks. *(To* **Martha** *as* **Alice** *goes into cubicle)* The screws were all over me. They were watching my every move. I told you. I managed to get a call into Harry. Holy Harry. He's coming over. Pronto. Client privilege. If I can't sort this Martha, I'm holding you responsible.

Alice *comes out of cubicle.*

DELO: It's dog eat dog out there, Alice. You'd need eyes in the back of your head the way business is these days.

Alice *goes back into cubicle*

DELO: *(To* **Martha***)* That pox-faced young one from Drimnagh? Natalie Foran? Are you with me Martha? Ghandi Lee's so-called mot. She's only flooding the joint with gear. And where's she getting it? Freddie Roe! And where's he getting it? Elementary. It has to be Harry. Holy Harry. The slimy …

Alice *comes back out of cubicle.*

DELO: I tell you, Alice, the world of multinational corporate finance has nothing on the machinations going on outside that door. You would not believe the treachery and backstabbing that goes on, would she Martha? Martha there, now she was my Vice President so to speak. Took early retirement. Before I finalized her pension plans. Tut tut. Very sad.

MARTHA: Lay off of me.

ALICE: Leave her in peace. There's no call to be always on at her. The poor child has enough on her plate.

DELO: Sau-cy. You're going to mind her, eh? You're going to nursemaid her? Don't make me laugh. I know this young one. Nearly two-and-a-half years we've been in this cell together. Haven't we? Haven't we?

MARTHA: Yes, but …

DELO: Then this blow-in comes along, golden fanny herself, Mrs Butter-wouldn't-melt! — our friendship means nothing? *(***Delo*** clocks the fact that pill is gone)* Ve-ry interestink. This should be a bit of fun.

MARTHA: I'm only trying to keep myself together. I'm only doing me best. I don't want any trouble.

DELO: Trips Unlimited. That's me. Going where no one else dares. Ha. When push comes to shove who stands by you? Slackarse there, according to herself, mind you, is going to be out any day. She's been singing that song all month since she came in to this cell. What about when Jasmine made her communion? Huh? Who dressed her? Did I ask for a penny back? Did I? Or the wreath? That time your Uncle Joe died? Eh? Didn't I always throw a few bob your way? Over and above? And looka — *(Going to* **Martha** *s locker)* doggy woggy here, woof woof. Thanks Delo, says Doggy. Ooh this smells nice. Thanks Delo for the lovely perfume. Snuff snuff. And mmmn face cream! Clinique! Turn Around Cream! You'd need a fucking atomic bomb to turn that sourpuss around.

MARTHA: I know. But. I mean …

DELO: There are young ones out there'd give their eye teeth to be sharing with Delo Roche.

ALICE: You're a wicked woman, Dolores Roche.

DELO: You stay out of this, manure head.

ALICE: No. I'll speak my mind. I see what you're up to. You've blood on your hands and you know it.

DELO: *I ve* blood on my hands? *I* have? That's rich.

Silence. **Martha** *gets up and does stretching exercises.*

MARTHA: Take a breath. Hold it. Let it go. Take a breath. Hold it. Let it go. Take a breath. Hold it. Let it go. Take a breath. Hold it. Let it go. Take a breath. Hold it. Let it go.

DELO: Shut it. I can't hear myself think.

Martha *continues exercises in silence.*

DELO: I said shut it.

MARTHA: I'm not saying a word.

DELO: Just stop. You're in me space.

MARTHA: I'll do them over here.

DELO: I said shut the fuck. I can hear you thinking. I can hear you both thinking. *(Screams)* Stop thinking!

MARTHA: I …

DELO: That's it pox face. Come on now. Tell it to Snakey. *(**Delo** whips off top and grabs **Martha** by hair forcing her to her knees)*

DELO: Here Snakey, Martha has a little confession to make. Tell Snakey Martha. Martha here's fallen in love. That must be it. With a psychopath. She won't even give me a sniff of her gee anymore. Wince, wince. Too crude for you Alice? I'll give you crude. You're welcome to her. The whore's melt. And in this case, Ms Casey, it's not just the vernacular! Her mother would let anyone do her for a fiver. Did you know that? Oh famous she was. That's why all the Casey's are different, Snakey. Red, black, brown, blonde — oh the Casey's could teach us all a thing or too about bio-diversity. Her mother did more single-handedly, or should that be single-cuntedly, to expand the gene pool of the Irish nation … Oh Martha doesn't lick it off the stones Snakey. What's she got that I haven't? Tell that to Snakey?

*Delo whacks **Martha** a few times around head and pushes her down onto chair.*

DELO: We're too good for her Snakey.

MARTHA: Too good! You're a stinking old woman. The smell off you makes me sick. Do you hear? It turns me stomach. And it was the same for Lila. She couldn't stand the stink of you. She bleached her fingers after you. Do you know what she told me in the dream? No? She killed herself rather than put up with the smell of you. She wanted me to tell you that.

Silence.

DELO: *(Taking pair of knickers out of her pocket and waving them at **Alice**)* Are these yours Alice? This is the smell you're getting Martha. The same smell as Annie. Yes! That's it! You're just another knacker.

ALICE: *(Attempting to grab at knickers)* Give them back to me.

DELO: Get away from them. Sniff. Sniff. That's what you were smelling Martha. Dead fish. Dead fucking fish.

ALICE: They're my property.

DELO: Ooh. Touch-y. Mother Macree's getting excited.

ALICE: You're an ignorant woman.

*Delo grabs **Alice** by the front of her blouse and in her face —*

DELO: Repeat that!

Delo shaking her —

DELO: Say it again! To me face!

ALICE: You – are – an – ignorant – woman. Now. I'm not afraid of you. Though you're steeped in death. It hangs around you like a cloud.

DELO: You're the one's in for killing.

ALICE: I killed cleanly, in self-defence. I don't have the blood of my own children on my hands. Paris! Spain!

DELO: What did you say?

ALICE: Yes! Killed them. As good as. Overdose. Suicide. Who gave them the gear? Who got them started on the stuff? Now. Take your filthy hands off me.

*Delo hits her a box. **Alice** goes reeling. **Martha** jumps on **Delo**'s back trying to restrain her. **Delo**'s rage increases, she shakes*

Martha off. Alice winds up cowering by locker at end of bunks and Martha winds up cowering in bunk in a foetal crouch. Delo screams, long howl of pain.

DELO: I'm surrounded by snakes in the grass. I've no space to think. I can't hear myself think. You and your fucking embroidery. And that sleeveen. Martha Casey. A turncoat. A fucking spy. Filling the bogwoman's head with lies. It is you, isn't it, started the rumours? You told her, didn't you?

DELO *(Takes out knife and waves it about)* Get over there. Out of my space. Get. Now. That's better.

Delo puts knife away and takes up Alice's crochet. Rips some out and with wool begins to divide the cell in two.

DELO: This is my space over here. That's yours. In future you'll stay over there and we'll all be just hunky dory.

MARTHA: That's Alice's wool. She needs it.

DELO: Tough tit.

ALICE: Leave her, child. It's only wool.

MARTHA: What about the door? And the water?

DELO: Ask and permission may or indeed may not be granted.

MARTHA: It's not fair.

DELO: Fair? Don't make me laugh.

MARTHA: There's two of us on this side. If anything we should have the bigger space.

DELO: Ah but there's potentially two of us over here. Do you see? You could move over.

MARTHA: I'm not sleeping in Lila's bunk.

DELO: We could swop the bunks around. Bring those over here and …

MARTHA: Then I'd be in Annie's bunk. No fucking way.

DELO: My but we're superstitious.

MARTHA: This is mad. It's still not fair.

DELO: At any second we could be joined by a fourth person. So technically the cell is divided fairly. Couldn't be fairer. And since I am the longest serving member of the club — four years I've resided here — I figure a couple of perks are in order. Anyway what are either of you going to do about it?

ALICE: It's absurd.

VOICE: Solicitor to see Dolores Roche. Dolores Roche.

DELO: And fuck you too. Whoever you are.

Buzzer sounds and door opens. Exit **Delo**.

Silence. Then sobbing from **Martha**.

ALICE: You're alright. Are you alright?

Martha *is staring intently at her palm.*

ALICE: I think Dolores is losing it. Up here.

Silence.

MARTHA: I didn't take anything. I swear.

Silence.

MARTHA: I'm sorry.

ALICE: How a body can stand it I don't know. We'll have to do something. You couldn't go on like this. Day in day out year after year. Are you alright, daughter?

MARTHA: *(Going up)* I just saw the colours. Did you ever see anything like that. Look! Can you not see it Alice. It's just … fuck sake. Look!

ALICE: I need a cup of tea.

MARTHA: *(Down on floor)* Jesus. Look at that — will you look — *(Laughing)*

ALICE: Martha, get up child. You took something, didn't you? What did she give you?

MARTHA:*(Laughing)* Mastermind. What colour is this? Like goo goo. Goo goo in here. Goo goo out there. Goo goo everywhere.

ALICE: Get a grip now, Martha.

MARTHA: Can you smell them — the colours. You should see your face. Oh Mammy. Alice?

ALICE: *(Shaking **Martha**)* Listen to me! Do you know the road to Kilnagros? Sure how could you know it. I've a bit of bog there. I like to work the bog in my bare feet. You'd come home and your feet would be brown as nuts. You'd get a mad feeling of freedom. As if you were a girl all over again with not a worry in the world. I'd been footing the turf that day and … Are you alright, daughter?

MARTHA: Please. I don't …

ALICE: Some stories are better left untold. My mother used say that. I didn't believe her then.

*Silence. **Alice** begins to unpick cell division and wind the wool back into a ball as she tells the following story.*

ALICE: I was putting the hens in for the night. Mac started a terrible racket up at the house, barking out of him. And then nothing. Christ that silence was bad. I knew it was bad. I stayed where I was. Now the hens I keep in an old byre. It's like a museum of agriculture in there. There's stuff going back — tools and farm implements, all rusted of course. I took down a sickle off the wall and I waited. I was hoping he'd —

MARTHA: Who?

ALICE: Shamy McGrane, the man I killed.

MARTHA: Go on. I'm sweating. Buckets. Can you see it?

ALICE: I was hoping he'd go away. I was thinking the kettle on the range would be nearly boilt and with a bit of luck he'd be gone before it boilt dry. And I was worrying about Mac. Next thing Shamy is in the doorway. The hens got up a fierce racket and the cock went for him. Chantyclare — that was the cock's name, a beautiful bird. If ever there was a gorgeous fowl it was Chantyclare. Well the cock was running on him, scrawbing at him. And Shamy got a hold on him and wrung his neck. He hadn't seen me yet. And I don't know what came over me, or where I got the strength from but I went for him with the sickle. In the eye I pierced him. The point broke off, it was that rusted. Sticking out of his eye. He was mad. Oh I tell you he was mad. Crazy with the poitín and half-blinded by the sickle, he came at me. And I gave him an unmerciful kick in the ... testicles. He fell back screaming. And when he was down on his back I took the sock of an old plough from the corner and walloped him three times across the head. And he was dead.

MARTHA: Jesus. What did you do?

ALICE: I went up to the house and had a cup of tea. Mac was a goner, God love him. I don't remember thinking it out but by the end of the second cup I had a plan. It was dark at this stage. But I know every blade of grass, even in the dark. I got the wheelbarrow and I got him into it. Christ knows where I got the strength. He was the dead weight of

a bull. I pushed him as far as the deep ditch between the
two back fields and tipped him into it. You'd need to be
looking very hard to find him in there. I cleaned the
henhouse out. The hay was drenched with his blood but it
would make great compost I knew and it'd rot down fast for
I have a dinger of a compost heap I can tell you. Then I
buried Mac in the orchard near to a sweet apple, a young
tree. It hadn't even fruited yet. Then I had a long bath with
Radox in it. Every bone in my body was aching.

MARTHA: Oh Mammy.

ALICE: I kept my fingers crossed no one had seen him
come over to my place. And sure if they did what of it? He
was on his own. His boozing cronies weren't going to get
off their arses to look for him. And he was always
disappearing up Arigna way on the batter. He'd people,
distant cousins I think, up Sliabh Anieran, all mad as
himself and inbred. He'd go up there betimes persecuting
them. So I knew I'd a few day's grace. I was worried about
the smell. To be honest I was most anxious about polluting
the river. That was what I was really afraid of, for I loved
that river. Ah it was only a stream really, but the ditch
drained into it, do you see, and I thought his putrefacting
body would poison it.

MARTHA: Oh Mammy.

ALICE: Aye it was creepy alright. There wasn't a word
about him for three days and then Mikey, the postman,
made an inquiry. Casual. The way you would. Oh says I, I
haven't seen sight nor sound of him. Not a lie. But I figured
now that the curiosity of the neighbours would be getting
up and wasn't I the stupid woman that didn't make a better
plan? I thought in the back of my mind that seeing as he
was in the deep ditch and it all covered over with brambles
— sure you couldn't see into it at all even in the heart of
winter when the quicks were bare — that my secret would
be safe. A couple of nights later I dumped a load of lime on

him to keep the smell down and I went about my business.
Of course Mikey was wild curious about Mac. I just told
him he'd passed away and I didn't have to feign my sorrow
for in truth I was heartbroken. And the next thing I knew
didn't Mikey in the goodness of his heart arrive along with
a new dog for me. A peculiar mixed up yoke it was too.
Very highly strung — a mix of a lurcher and a setter and
God knows what else. Talk of inbred. A terrible conundrum
of bits. No, I told him. I was finished with dogs but he
insisted. And it seemed like bad grace to refuse and by this
time the guards were looking for Shamy and the theory was
he'd fallen drunk into some hidey hole or drowned in the
lake at Kesh. So I held on to the dog and faith if it didn't
fixate on the deep ditch. A good nose is right. I'd to keep
him locked up day and night for as soon as he had his way
he was up to the very spot and barking and whimpering out
of him. Me, I just kept me head down and prayed it would
all blow over.

MARTHA: So how did they twig?

ALICE: The cursed lurcher. Up he runs the tail wagging
like billio and Shamy's foot in his mouth and the leg trailing
after him the length of the body. He was delighted with
himself.

MARTHA: It sounds like something out of a horror movie.

Martha bends double with cramps.

MARTHA: Here we go again.

ALICE: Mikey knew rightly what the leg meant. The stink
of it you would not credit.

MARTHA: Give us a break. I feel really weird Alice. Look
at my hands.

ALICE: I'm not finished!

MARTHA: I'm not going to get through this.

ALICE: Mikey came back with the guards.

MARTHA: What the fuck are you on about? You have me brain sore with your talk. You have no idea what it's like. You have no idea at all.

ALICE: Haven't you your beautiful daughter to live for. Her life is only beginning.

MARTHA: The truth is I'm not even allowed access. Bastards. They gave Jasmine to his Ma. The wagon. The lies she told the social worker. Okay, I was strung out. But not that bad. I'd never hurt my baby. Not on purpose. It was a total accident. She just wouldn't shut up. She bawled her head off for a week. My body feels really strange. I feel huge …

ALICE: But at least she's with her father.

Martha shakes head — No.

ALICE: Didn't you tell me she's with her Daddy?

MARTHA: He's dead. The virus.

ALICE: When did this happen?

MARTHA: I was only in a couple of months. They wouldn't even let me out to the funeral. Bastards. *(Screaming)* Bastards. He was a scumbag. Oh shit. I don't know what's happening to me.

Martha weeps. Alice comforts her.

ALICE: Hush. Hush. Child of grace. It's not fair what some have to bear.

MARTHA: I didn't mean to say those things.

ALICE: Never speak ill of the dead. That was another saying of my mother's. God rest her soul. But now I don't know, Martha. Maybe we should speak ill of them if they deserve it. So the truth gets told.

MARTHA: I can't go on.

ALICE: Hush. Child. Hush.

MARTHA: I can't go on. I keep thinking of Lila. I swear Alice she does be around me. And I even think I do be seeing Annie and then I think there must have been someone before Annie, don't you know, and I think I can see *her* sometimes. And then before her, whoever she was, there'd be someone else and on and on and on forever until the time they built this prison. And we're all trapped here — the living and the dead alike. Do you understand? And I do think I'll be next. That they're all waiting for me just over there. In a world just beside this one. Like you could put your hand out and touch them they're that close. And I think it'd be alright then to die. Like it would be good. And not bad the way they say it is to take your own life. Do you understand Alice?

Door buzzer sounds.

VOICE: Social worker to see Martha Casey. Social worker to see Martha Casey.

MARTHA: I'm not taking it.

ALICE: Don't be a fool. Go out and see what she wants. It might be news about Jasmine. You have to go out.

MARTHA: I'm afraid. It might be a trap.

ALICE: You can't be afraid for ever.

Door buzzer sounds and door opens.

ALICE: *(Shouting)* Get out there for God's sake. Now. Now. *(Going to speaker)* She's coming. She coming now.

Alice bundles **Martha** *over to door. Exit* **Martha.**

ALICE: I hope I did the right thing.

She climbs up onto **Delo***'s bunk and looks out window.*

ALICE: *(Singing)*

> *Now come all you good people, and I hope you'll lend an ear,*
> *The travels of an old cow I mean to let you hear,*
> *You could not get a match for her and search through every fair,*
> *She was reared by Pat O'Hurry who lived near Ballinaglair.*
> *He brought her out to Dowray and many another fair,*
> *And then unto Drumkeerin and also Dromahaire*
> *Along to Knockarena then on to Ballysadare*
> *And then unto Drumshanbo, but he couldn't sell her there.*
> *He took her down near Sligo to a place called Ballinode ...*

Oh Holy Mother!

Buzzer sounds. Door opens. **Delo** *enters. She catches* **Alice** *climbing down off bunk.*

DELO: What were you doing snooping up there?

ALICE: I was just having a look out the window.

DELO: A free look!

ALICE: There's no law against it.

DELO: You're wrong there Mother Macree. It's enshrined in the law of cell twenty-seven. The bunk belongs to me; the view belongs to me. My side; your side. Capisco? Remember? Now as an expert in legal affairs, shall we say, you should be very clued in on the law. *(Assuming* **Martha** *is in cubicle)* Amn't I right Martha? Eh?

Silence.

DELO: Are you gone deaf Martha Casey!

Silence.

DELO: Sulking are we?

ALICE: Martha's out on a visit.

DELO: What? You let her out? You fool!

ALICE: She had a visit.

DELO: And she took it? Who is it?

ALICE: I don't know.

DELO: Who's Martha seeing? Hmmn?

ALICE: I don't know.

DELO: Don't know? Won't tell!

Delo *gets bottle of vodka and pours drink.*

DELO: Care to join me? No? That's a mite unneighbourly, as they say in the Westerns.

ALICE: I want nothing from you, Dolores Roche.

DELO: Except me view.

ALICE: Stop goading me.

DELO: Listen cunt, let's get a few things straight around here. Just because you poisoned, yes poisoned, Martha's heart against me doesn't give you any right to be so high and bleeding mighty. I'm a forgiving sort of woman. But some things are just too close to the bone. Martha and me and Lila — we had something special, really special.

ALICE: I've been minding my own business.

DELO: That's good. Priceless. What exactly is your business? The cutlery trade is it? *(She laughs)*

ALICE: This conversation has come to an end.

DELO: Butchery.

Silence.

DELO: Butchery. The name and the game. I have it here. All about you.

DELO: *(Takes folded newspaper cutting from pocket, waves it under **Alice**'s nose)* Poor old woman persecuted by sex-crazed neighbour. I think not. Would the word skeleton ring a bell. Hmm?

ALICE: It were lies. Every word of it.

DELO: You building yourself up as a sainted put-upon innocent. Wisha, wisha, wisha. And to think I let you make the tea. Everything changes now. Oh yes bejaysus it does.

***Alice** grabs cutting and tears it to shreds. **Delo** laughs at her.*

DELO: You're pathetic. I can see I'm going to have a long chat with Martha. Tell her the facts of life. Fact number one, never turn your back on Mother Macree.

ALICE: I just want to be left in peace. Martha just wants to be left in peace.

DELO: That's a laugh. Martha'll be just hitting the screaming benders round about now.

ALICE: Martha's doing her best to put her life back together and it's helping her you should be. She's young enough to be one of your daughters and from what I hear you're doing your best to drive her to a similar end.

DELO: Let me tell you one thing for your edification, Mrs Cuntface — Martha's already lost. A write off. By now she won't be sure of her own name. She'll be somewhere west of Pluto. And she'll come crashing down looking for any bit of comfort she can get. And it won't be you she'll want it from.

ALICE: What are you talking about?

DELO: Martha's in orbit. The first Irishwoman in space. *(Laughs)* You don't get it, do you?

Buzzer sounds and door opens.

DELO: Prepare for re-entry!

Martha *Enters looking seriously disoriented. She makes her way about the cell examining objects as if seeing them for the first time. She stares at her hands.* **Delo** *and* **Alice** *look on,* **Alice** *baffled.*

ALICE: Martha. Martha child, what is it? Are you …

DELO: *(Laughs)* The floorshow is about to begin.

ALICE: Don't pay her any heed. Christ daughter what is it?

DELO: This should pass a happy hour or so. The main event.

Martha *begins to feel* **Alice***'s face as if she were a blind woman.*

MARTHA: Nothing stays still. All shifts. Nothing. Not for a moment. Still. All moves.

DELO: Opportunity knocks.

ALICE: Do you know me Martha? Do you remember me?

MARTHA: I said mother. The woman … the woman …

ALICE: The social worker was it?

DELO: *There was an old woman who lives in the woods, weela weela wiyla, There was an old woman who lived in the woods down by the river side-a …*

MARTHA: Mother. *(Little girl's voice)* My mother's voice. My mother's heart. My mother said. My mother said come home. Come home. The dark and rain. Come. My mother said come. The dark.

DELO: Cootchy-cootchy. Come here Martha.

ALICE: Get your hands off her.

DELO: Martha! Have I got news for you baby. Mother Macree ain't who you thought she was …

ALICE: No.

They are pulling **Martha** *between them.*

ALICE: Leave her go.

DELO: You leave her go.

MARTHA: *(Shaking herself loose from both of them — in a singsong voice)* Because. Because. Because. One for Mammy. One for Martha. One for Baby. One for Mammy. One for Martha. One for Baby. And other one for Martha.

ALICE: You gave her the drugs. What did you give her? What's she on?

DELO: Will you ever cop onto yourself missus? She's flipped.

ALICE: She needs help.

DELO: She's fine. Sit back and watch the show. It's only the moon.

ALICE: Look at her eyes.

MARTHA: I was afraid of the worms coming up through the sand. And Mammy carried me over. She said they weren't worms at all. Only the air pushing up and making the shapes of worms.

ALICE: What happened out there? What did the social worker say?

MARTHA: And Mammy carried me over. Look she said. It's only sand in the shape of a worm. And she carried me over and put me down into the water. She promised she'd buy me an ice-cream. And she didn't. *(Coming back to her own voice)* I want my baby. I want her.

Alice goes to speaker at door

ALICE: Hello. Hello. Is there anybody there?

DELO: Get away from that fucking door.

ALICE: Hello. Is there anybody hearing me?

DELO: *(Pulling knife. Slowly)* I said get-away-from-the-door.

MARTHA: I want my baby. Give me back my …

ALICE: Will nobody help us?

DELO: Just shift. Over there. Now.

ALICE: Put it down Dolores. Please.

MARTHA: I didn't mean to hurt her. I didn't mean it.

DELO: I've had enough of you.

Martha is behind Delo. She reaches across and takes knife from Delo's hand. Scuffle ensues. Three women are locked together in struggle. Blackout during which we hear Delo say in a low voice:

DELO: Martha. Lila. Martha.

Lights up on cell. Four hours later. Night through window and strange greenish cell light. Body of Delo is on floor covered with blanket off spare bunk. Martha slumped dozing in a chair. Alice in other chair, alert, drinking tea. Martha comes round.

MARTHA: I'm afraid.

ALICE: Yes.

MARTHA: They'll never let me out now.

ALICE: They will.

MARTHA: Jesus. I'll never see my little girl.

ALICE: Yes, you will.

MARTHA: What's going to happen to me?

ALICE: Nothing.

MARTHA: That's easy for you to say.

ALICE: Go and put on a jumper. You're very cold.

MARTHA: *(To body)* I'm afraid. Of …

ALICE: *(Laughing)* She can't harm you now, child.

MARTHA: I dozed off again.

ALICE: And why wouldn't you? Aren't you exhausted?

MARTHA: I'm sorry. Was I long asleep?

ALICE: Hardly a minute, child. Get into the bunk bed, why don't you?

MARTHA: What'll we do?

ALICE: I'm puzzling that one out.

MARTHA: How long have we got?

ALICE: A few hours yet.

*Alice fetches quilt and drapes it around **Martha**.*

MARTHA: I can't believe I did it.

ALICE: Did what, child?

MARTHA: Did what? Did what? What the fuck do you think I'm talking about?

ALICE: *(Holding up knife with handkerchief)* There are three sets of fingerprints on this knife. I didn't wipe them for to the mind of the police that would be suspicious and incriminatory. There's Dolores'. There's yours. And there's mine.

MARTHA: What are you getting at?

ALICE: You, Martha, were on drugs. You were very confused and shocked by the whole thing. And well you might be for it was a horrific occurrence.

MARTHA: What are you saying?

ALICE: I never knew a child for such questions. What I'm saying is that in your confusion, out, as you were, of your mind on whatever drugs that evil and wretched woman had given to you, you even at one point thought *you* had killed her. Isn't that a quare thing?

MARTHA: But …

ALICE: Whereas I was stone cold sober in my own fully conscious mind and completely aware of what happened …

MARTHA: But …

ALICE: Which is exactly as I am about to tell you now. So listen very carefully to me Martha Casey.

MARTHA: But I …

ALICE: Fuck it Martha. Concentrate! And don't interrupt! You came back from your visit. You weren't feeling too good. You'd been trying to stay off drugs and Dolores Roche had given you something that she said would help the symptoms of withdrawal. But it was some powerful mind-altering substance. You're with me so far? When you

came into the cell a row was in progress between Alice
Kane and Dolores Roche. You don't know what it was
about but Dolores would regularly goad both you and Alice
and use any excuse to provoke a row. And here you might
even mention Lila, and Annie before her, and the way they
died. Or were driven to take their own lives. The row hotted
up. Dolores Roche produced a knife. There is no doubt she
would have used it. Alice Kane managed to grab it from
her. Dolores Roche fell and Alice Kane stabbed her. A pity
she fell on her front. Stab wounds in the back always have
bad associations. She died. You picked up the knife. That'll
explain your prints on it. You were in a state of deep shock
and confusion so you cannot be expected to remember
every little detail. But you'll remember what I've just told
you?

MARTHA: I can't do it.

ALICE: Yes you can; and yes you will.

MARTHA: Why are you doing this?

ALICE: I don't rightly know daughter. What have I to
lose? Now there's a question you won't be asking. And I
won't be answering. Call it the figaries of a poor country
woman. It'll be the dawn in a few hours. It won't feel so
bad then. Things never do, in the morning light. This whole
episode is so familiar to me: like I saw it once in a dream or
I lived through it once in another life. This cell; you there
daughter with your sorrow-filled face; poor Dolores dead on
the floor. Even the palms of my own hands with her life's
blood on them. Poor Dolores.

*Alice climbs up on **Delo**'s bunk and looks out window.*

ALICE: Such a huge moon. Magnificent. There's frost over
everything! It's amazing Martha. The whole world is turned
to crystal. All the roofs are white. The new prison is like a
big ferry sailing across the sky. And Lila's tree has turned to

pure silver in the moonlight. Glittery and shiny. It's a Christmas tree for sure. Come up and see. Come up Martha. It's so beautiful it would take your breath away.

Blackout.

THE END